Evaluating
Performance

BEST PRACTICES:
Evaluating Performance

HOW TO APPRAISE, PROMOTE, AND FIRE

BARRY SILVERSTEIN

Collins

An Imprint of HarperCollins Publishers

Employment laws differ from state to state. The editors
recommend consulting your company's human resources
or legal department before taking any action regarding
employees.

Produced for HarperCollins by:

HYLAS PUBLISHING
129 MAIN STREET
IRVINGTON, NY 10533
WWW.HYLASPUBLISHING.COM

FIRST EDITION
Library of Congress Cataloguing-in-Publication Data has
been applied for.

ISBN: 978-0-06-114560-5
ISBN-10: 0-06-114560-2

07 08 09 10 11   RRD   10 9 8 7 6 5 4 3 2

Barry Silverstein is a business writer and management consultant. He has 30 years of experience managing and motivating people in small and large businesses. He founded his own direct and Internet marketing agency and ran it for 20 years, growing it to a $5 million, 50-person organization. He has also held management positions with Xerox Corporation and advertising agency Arnold Worldwide.

Silverstein is the author of three titles in the Collins Best Practices series. He is also the coauthor of *The Breakaway Brand* (McGraw-Hill, 2005) and the author of *Business-to-Business Internet Marketing* (Maximum Press, 2001) and *Internet Marketing for Information Technology Companies* (Maximum Press, 2001).

Contents

Preface

What has proven to be the best way to assess an employee's performance? How can you turn around an underperformer? How do you know when an employee is ready to be promoted? What issues should be considered before firing an employee? Is there any way to make the performance review process less burdensome?

In this book, we distill the wisdom of some of the best minds in the field of performance management to help you evaluate employees and manage their work more effectively. The language is simple and the design colorful to make the information easy to grasp.

Quizzes help you assess your knowledge of performance-management issues. Case files show how companies have tackled tough performance issues. Sidebars give you a big-picture look at evaluating, promoting, and firing employees and highlight innovative, out-of-the-box solutions worth considering. Quotes from business leaders will motivate you as you hone your performance-management skills. Finally, in case you want to dig deeper into the topic of performance evaluation and related management issues, we recommend some of the most important business books available. The authors of these books both influence and reflect today's thinking about evaluating employees and related issues. Understanding the ideas they cover will inspire you as a manager.

Even if you don't dip into these volumes, the knowledge you gain from studying the pages of this book will equip you to deal effectively and insightfully with performance management issues every day—to help you make a difference to your company and in the lives of the people who support you.

THE EDITORS

ONE-ON-ONE PERFORMANCE MANAGEMENT

> "The best way to inspire people to superior performance is to convince them by everything you do and by your everyday attitude that you are wholeheartedly supporting them."
>
> —Harold S. Geneen,
> CEO of ITT
> (1910–1997)

With today's shifting workforce, a manager's responsibility for evaluating employees is all the more challenging and complex. In the coming years, as more and more baby boomers retire, experienced workers will be at a premium as they become increasingly hard to find.

Self-Assessment Quiz

HOW WELL DO YOU MANAGE YOUR EMPLOYEES' PERFORMANCE?

Read each of the following statements and indicate whether you agree or disagree. Then check your score at the end.

1. I get to know each of my employee's likes and dislikes.

   ○ Agree   ○ Disagree

2. I generally can tell when an employee is distracted or having trouble focusing on the job.

   ○ Agree   ○ Disagree

3. Employees generally trust me.

   ○ Agree   ○ Disagree

4. I evaluate an employee's performance at least quarterly.

   ○ Agree   ○ Disagree

5. I often informally let my employees know how they are doing, in addition to giving scheduled evaluations.

   ○ Agree   ○ Disagree

6. I tell employees when they are doing something wrong, but I try to present my comments as constructive criticism.

   ○ Agree   ○ Disagree

7. Employees know that they can tell me something personal and it will remain confidential.

   ◯ Agree   ◯ Disagree

8. I believe in promoting from within when it is possible to do so.

   ◯ Agree   ◯ Disagree

9. I encourage employees to speak their minds, and I really listen to what they have to say.

   ◯ Agree   ◯ Disagree

10. I would not terminate an employee for poor performance without giving ample opportunity to correct the problem.

    ◯ Agree   ◯ Disagree

Scoring

Give yourself 1 point for every question you answered "Agree" and 0 points for every question you answered "Disagree."

Analysis

8–10	You manage your employees' performance very well.
5–7	You need to work on your performance management skills.
0–4	You have a lot more to learn if you want to be a good manager of employee performance.

Most companies will hire younger employees with fewer years on the job—individuals who need well-defined goals, on-the-job training, and continual supervision.

What should managers look for when they evaluate the performance of these employees? How should they evaluate an individual employee's initiative, work quality, and potential for advancement? How should managers document employee evaluations? How often should they review employee performance? How do managers promote an employee—or fire one?

There are no shortcuts to employee evaluation, but there are processes, strategies, and techniques that help managers evaluate employees more effectively. This book addresses the fundamentals of employee evaluation: hiring, day-to-day performance management, reviews, and what to do about performance problems.

WHY PERFORMANCE MANAGEMENT MATTERS

Traditionally, evaluating performance has meant employee appraisal, or "the performance review." Today, however, many organizations are moving beyond simply reviewing employee performance toward a more comprehensive performance-management process.

Performance management is a process-oriented approach to evaluating and supporting employees. Ideally, performance management takes place from the moment the employee is hired to fill a position at a company to the moment the individual leaves the organization.

If a company and its management adopt this broad view, managers are in a much better position to help develop each employee's potential, and employees feel better about their positions and the company they work for.

Performance management helps managers develop the staff they have and keep them motivated; raise the standards of quality and promote productivity; and keep employees in tune with corporate goals.

At the heart of performance management is the process of employee evaluation. Ideally, managers periodically evaluate employees informally throughout the year; formal evaluations typically are done on a quarterly or annual basis.

In fact, the annual performance appraisal has stirred up controversy in management circles. Although the performance appraisal is intended to help employees improve their performance, succeed at their jobs, and then potentially be

The BIG Picture

EVALUATIONS VERSUS APPRAISALS

Performance "appraisal" is often mistaken for performance "evaluation." An appraisal is typically conducted once a year and is usually connected to compensation (that is, salary increases and bonuses). Managers and employees alike often find the appraisal process burdensome and dissatisfying.

promoted, it often ends up being used merely as an annual review—a method of handing out rewards and punishments. This is why current opinion favors using the performance appraisal as just one element of the broader performance-management process, which encompasses the employee's entire tenure at the company from hire onward.

Constructive performance evaluations can yield significant benefits. In fact, they may be

Outside the Box

A PERFORMANCE AND VALUES MATRIX

Former General Electric CEO Jack Welch described four types of employees in a letter to shareholders in the company's 1991 annual report. He wrote that the two types that are easiest to spot are employees who delivered on commitments and shared the company's values and employees who did not meet commitments or share values. The third type were employees who shared values but failed to meet commitments. Welch felt these individuals could be redirected. The fourth type, however, was the most problematic: those who delivered on commitments but did not share corporate values. Ultimately, Welch sent them packing.

You can create a performance and values matrix to help you evaluate your employees in a similar way. Think about the employee's only opportunity to spend individual time with a supervisor. The more often they occur, the better the communication will be between manager and employee, which improves morale. When supervisors make time for frequent evaluations, several key benefits can result:

Job satisfaction. Job satisfaction tends to increase after a review, because the employee is getting personal attention from the manager and is involved in the evaluation process.

the people on your staff and whether they perform well and share company values. Then place them into the appropriate boxes on this matrix:

PERFORMANCE	VALUES
High	High
Mixed	Mixed
Low	Low

As you evaluate employees, consider the specific events and behaviors that guided your decision of where to place them in the matrix. Then, for each person, identify weak areas, decide if coaching is needed, and devise a plan to help the person improve.

SOURCE: *The Leadership Engine* by Noel M. Tichy (HarperCollins, 1997).

Improved performance. If the manager delivers feedback in a positive way and both employee and manager agree to specific goals, a significant improvement in performance can result.

Development. Performance evaluations offer excellent opportunities for managers and staff to agree on how workers' abilities can be developed—whether through formal or on-the-job training or skills-development programs.

Rewards and recognition. When performance evaluations are linked with rewards and recognition, and are used as the basis for salary increases and bonuses, they become even more powerful motivators.

Organizational improvement. Performance evaluations can provide a valuable assessment of how certain types of people perform in specific jobs. Managers can use this information to improve job descriptions and to recruit the person best suited for a position.

START BY HIRING THE RIGHT PEOPLE

The first step in performance management is hiring the right person for the right job. All too often, a manager is forced to hire under pressure. When an employee leaves a position, or when a new job opens up, the manager scrambles to fill the opening as soon as possible. In the heat of the moment, the manager might settle for a conveniently available job candidate instead of waiting for the best-qualified one.

While it may be time consuming, you should thoroughly screen all viable candidates during the hiring process. Match the candidate's skill set

CASE *FILE*

HALLMARK DETERMINES IF NEW HIRES MEET EXPECTATIONS

When Hallmark Cards couldn't find a tool to help it measure its recruiting success, the company built its own "staffing index." New employees were scored on "initial candidate quality" from average to outstanding. After six months on the job, the employee was evaluated on the same five-point scale to determine if the manager's expectations had been realized. The process continued through the employee's first and second annual reviews, so the company's recruiters could get a long-term picture and "judge the enduring quality of a recent hire."

SOURCE: "Hallmark's Quality-of-Hire Initiative" by Aaron Dalton, *Workforce Management Online* (May 10, 2005).

to the position. Consider relevant experience and strong references, but also be sure the individual will fit well within your organization. You are actually evaluating the potential of the candidate to be successful at the job. This is just as important as employee evaluation.

What is the best way to get the right person for the job? Write the best job description possible.

The Job Description as a Performance Management Tool

A good job description is both a hiring blueprint and a performance management tool.

A job description should be written in concise, easy-to-understand language. It should include enough detail to convey specific job responsibilities, but be flexible enough to allow for employee growth.

Include the title of the job, a summary of the position, the employee's manager or supervisor, a list of specific responsibilities, including supervisory duties if any, and specific qualifications for the position, such as education, experience, and character traits.

Include a statement covering your company's expectation of how employees should relate to coworkers and customers and how employee performance will be evaluated.

It is also a good idea to add information about the company's working hours, pay range, and benefits.

The well-written, comprehensive job description outlines the expectations for the job and also sets a standard for performance. If the job description clearly states job requirements—skills, initiative, and interactions with coworkers and other departments—it not only ensures that candidates will be qualified, it also becomes the manager's guide for managing and evaluating employee performance. You should be able to use the responsibilities section of a good job description as a checklist during periodic employee performance evaluations.

Setting Goals for New Employees

As a manager, your responsibility is to establish goals that launch new employees in the right direction. Goal setting tells employees what you expect them to accomplish and outlines how you measure success.

In the first week on the job, a new employee should meet with you to discuss the goals for the position. This is your opportunity to review the job description and make sure the employee

"One of my goals is to inspire people to be all that they can be and, hopefully, be a good example and teach some useful, interesting principles. Perhaps I can be the key that turns on the engine in their life, and then they can take their car where they want."

—Mark Victor Hansen,
author of *The One Minute Millionaire*

fully understands the job responsibilities and the reporting structure. Give the employee tips about who will be helpful and how to navigate through your organization.

This is also a good time to explain to new employees how their specific job objectives support your organization's strategic business objectives. Aligning personal objectives with business objectives helps employees understand their role in the larger organization and provides motivation. New employees will be all the more

Behind the Numbers

PERFORMANCE APPRAISAL TACTICS

A survey of 218 human resource leaders at companies with 2,500 or more employees revealed that only 5 percent of respondents are satisfied with how performance management is handled in their organizations. The areas most lacking, according to the respondents, were performance management as a retention tool and the performance management system's lack of integration with succession planning. The highest level of satisfaction was with how the process of performance management identified top performers.

SOURCE: "Performance Management Underperforms" by Gina Ruiz, *Workforce Management* (June 26, 2006).

motivated if you encourage their participation in the goal-setting process. Involve the employee not only in helping you establish goals, but also in suggesting how to achieve them. Your role as a manager is to guide the employee, but not to

• POWER POINTS •

DAY-TO-DAY PERFORMANCE MANAGEMENT

These five basic steps will guide your day-to-day performance management:

- Plan what needs to be done, involve the employee in the planning process to encourage ownership of the tasks, and set expectations for the job.

- Monitor and periodically evaluate each employee's performance.

- Develop the individual's skills through training, challenging work, and opportunities for advancement.

- Review the employee's performance during quarterly or annual reviews using a rating scale or other form of objective measurement.

- Reward good performance with positive reinforcement.

provide step-by-step instructions for executing the job. Make it clear that the employee is a partner in success and will be held accountable for accomplishing the goals. Also discuss how success will be measured. Assure the employee that goal setting is flexible and that goals are reviewed periodically and collaboratively.

What to Measure

To evaluate job performance effectively, a manager must know what is important to measure. One way to approach measuring performance, popularized by management guru Peter Drucker, is management by objectives, sometimes known as the "MBO" method. In MBO, the manager establishes specific performance objectives, and the employee agrees to be judged by their successful completion. These objectives are individualized to an employee's position—the more specific the better. For example, an objective for a sales employee might be how many leads are generated in a defined period of time.

The primary benefit of the MBO method is that it measures outcomes objectively, instead of performance standards subjectively. The employee is actively involved in both setting the objectives and working to fulfill them. In effect, the employee self-manages and takes full responsibility for deciding how to accomplish each objective. While this provides the employee with a great deal of flexibility and independence, it can also be challenging and even intimidating, especially for younger or less experienced employees.

CASE *FILE*

FIRM USES PERFORMANCE MANAGEMENT IN TURNAROUND

In 1999, NCCI Holdings, a firm that provides data on workplace-injury claims, battled a takeover attempt, lost its strategic focus, and saw its employee turnover rate skyrocket. The HR staff studied the problem and decided to institute a new performance management system.

Under the new system, every employee's performance was tracked and then evaluated twice annually. Specific objectives were set and tied to compensation. The firm also instituted "360-degree evaluations," which rely on confidential feedback about the employee from coworkers and customers. Individualized coaching sessions were arranged for employees as needed.

Despite the complexity of implementing the new system, the effort paid off in large dividends. In two years, turnover decreased from more than 26 percent to 21 percent. Even more significant, NCCI retained 94 percent of the employees they identified as high performers.

SOURCE: "How Performance Management Reversed NCCI's Fortunes" by Patrick Kiger, *Workforce Management* (May 2002).

As a result, some companies use a performance rating system instead of the MBO method. In this method, the employee is rated on a series of

• POWER POINTS •

MEASURING EMPLOYEE PERFORMANCE

A variety of methods for rating employee performance have been developed:

Management by objectives – The manager establishes specific performance objectives and the employee agrees to be judged by their successful completion. Objectives are individualized to an employee's position.

Performance rating system – The employee is rated on a series of attributes, using an "Excellent" to "Poor" type of scale. Attributes can be generalized, such as attitude, effort, relationships, and communication skills, or they can be specific to the employee's position.

Narrative performance evaluation – Managers provide a narrative description of an employee's performance. The manager incorporates 360-degree feedback (confidential input from coworkers) into the narrative to provide a more complete picture of the employee's performance.

attributes using an "Excellent" to "Poor" type of scale. Attributes can be generalized, such as attitude, effort, relationships, and communication skills, or they can be specific to the employee's position. This appraisal method is less flexible than MBO, but it can be more easily standardized and therefore results can be analyzed across a company's entire workforce.

Other companies institute a modified rating system, which combines a rating scale with a narrative description of an employee's performance. The manager not only rates the employee on a scale, but also collects 360-degree feedback (confidential input from coworkers and customers) in a narrative to provide a more complete picture of the employee's performance. Sometimes the rating scale is combined with the MBO method by adding measurable objectives to the appraisal process.

The performance measurement method may vary based on your organization, but the measurement criteria are basically the same. Your goal as a manager is to measure the overall competence of your employees and their success in accomplishing the requirements of the position.

Setting Goals and Objectives

Whether or not you use management by objectives as a method of measuring employee performance, it is important to set goals and objectives for yourself and your employees. There is a fine line between goals and objectives, but there is a distinct difference: typically, a goal is a broader, more strategic end result that you or the organization wants to achieve, while an objective is a more narrowly defined, tactical result that supports the goal. For example, a corporate goal might be to "achieve undisputed

> "I'm able to bring business expertise but, more importantly, operating experience. The people here at Google are young. Every day there are lots of new challenges. I keep things focused. The speech I give every day is: "This is what we do. Is what you are doing consistent with that, and does it change the world?"
>
> Eric Schmidt,
> CEO of Google

leadership in the worldwide personal computer market this fiscal year," while an objective would be to "sell 100,000 personal computers in the first quarter of this fiscal year."

Setting goals and objectives provides direction and gives employees something to strive for. Just as important, it provides you as manager with a framework to evaluate performance. A common methodology for creating effective goals and objectives is the mnemonic "SMART," which stands for Specific, Measurable, Achievable, Realistic, and Time-related.

Behind the Numbers

EMPLOYEES NEED MORE POSITIVE REINFORCEMENT FOR THEIR PERFORMANCE

In recent employee surveys, half of the workers questioned said they received little or no credit for the jobs they perform, and nearly two-thirds said management is much more likely to offer negative criticism than praise for work well done. This should be a wake-up call to managers. By simply offering occasional praise and positive reinforcement, a manager could motivate employees to improve their performance.

These research findings are based on surveys of about 1.2 million employees at 52 primarily Fortune 1000 companies from 2001 to 2004.

SOURCE: "Stop Demotivating Your Employees!" by David Sirota et al., *Harvard Management Update* (January 2006).

Specific goals. When you set goals with an employee, be as specific as possible. The employee needs to know the type of goal, what resources and people may be needed, the date you expect the goal to be accomplished, and any other details.

Measurable goals. Establish how you will measure the successful completion of a goal. Criteria might include a due date, a percentage of improvement in quality, or a stipulated increase in quantity. Specifying what to measure at various stages before the final completion of the goal will help you monitor progress.

Achievable goals. Each goal should be motivational so that the employee feels compelled to act on it. In writing up the goal, use action words to energize the employee. Be sure the employee both understands and embraces the goal and is committed to achieving it. You as the manager must be willing to provide support.

Realistic goals. Ask yourself if the goal you set is realistic for the individual employee to accomplish. The employee may have other responsibilities, resources may be difficult to obtain, or organizational obstacles may get in the way. Reaching a realistic goal should be within the employee's control rather than dependent on many others. There is nothing wrong with setting a challenging goal—you want the employee to reach higher—but make sure it is attainable.

Time-related goals. An effective goal has an achievable end date. An end date establishes a timeline for the employee, reduces procrastination, and leads to a sense of accomplishment.

If the goal has an end date that projects beyond several months, it is also a good idea to help the employee establish interim dates for the completion of different phases.

Providing Frequent Feedback

There is little value in hiring employees, investing in training, acclimating them to your organization, and then letting them "sink or swim." And yet some managers take a hands-off approach and believe it is entirely up to the employee to succeed or fail.

This type of management style makes it difficult to evaluate an employee's performance

The BIG Picture

ORDINARY PEOPLE

Usually only 20 percent or less of your employees will be outstanding performers. This small percentage represents the few superstars who may exceed even your most ambitious objectives.

You should, of course, reward the outstanding performers, but be sure to recognize the "ordinary" performers as well. The 80 percent of your employees who work consistently, day in and day out, contributing in so many ways to your organization's success, are also important. Regular performance evaluations will reveal the efforts of these valuable but less visible employees.

because it handicaps even a competent employee from the start. Experienced managers recognize that employees need frequent feedback and positive reinforcement if they are to achieve their goals and perform to the best of their abilities.

This doesn't mean you have to hover over your employees, or supervise every detail of an employee's job. You can actually accomplish this easily with a simple technique: "Management By Walking Around" (MBWA). Over 20 years ago, Tom Peters and Robert H. Waterman, Jr., wrote about MBWA in their best-selling book, *In Search of Excellence.* This technique, which

CASE *FILE*

FREQUENT PERFORMANCE REVIEWS

A few years ago, managers at Whirlpool Corporation did most of their performance reviewing via computer. The system was put in place to ease what many had considered the onerous burden of reviewing employees. It wasn't long, however, before employees were complaining that they weren't getting enough feedback. So in 2004, Whirlpool revamped the process again.

Now, the company requires managers to review employees at least four times a year during face-to-face meetings. Whirlpool also stipulates that employees draft their own performance objectives, to

was used by senior managers at Hewlett-Packard to keep up their connection to their people, is still one of the best ways for managers to learn what's going on with their staff. You can apply it to your own situation, wherever you work.

Management By Walking Around literally means getting up, leaving your office, and making the rounds from one employee to another. By observing, asking questions, and, most important, listening, you can informally check up on how things are going. You can note how an employee is approaching a particular challenge, see problems as they are forming, and respond on the spot. Obviously, if the employees who report to you are scattered around the country

be reviewed by managers. One Whirlpool manager, who used to conduct reviews twice annually, decided to increase the frequency of his reviews to biweekly. He meets with his eight employees for up to 45 minutes each and says he has noticed "much better results."

According to the manager, the more frequent reviews keep him focused on coaching and developing his staff to expand their capabilities, which in turn allows him to delegate more work.

SOURCE: "For Relevance, Firms Revamp Worker Reviews" by Erin White, *Wall Street Journal* (July 17, 2006).

or the world, it may be logistically difficult to see every one of them, but you can substitute a casual phone conversation for face-to-face contact. However you do it, MBWA creates

CASE *FILE*

MUTUAL PERFORMANCE EXPECTATIONS

Sharp Electronics Company has developed a performance management process that you can emulate. Each manager is evaluated to assess strengths and to identify areas that need development. Once that assessment is complete, the immediate supervisor (typically a director) meets with each manager to review the results and to create individual plans to enhance each manager's performance. Sharp's performance management system strongly emphasizes evaluating employee performance based upon mutual expectations. This gives employees direct feedback about how performance results were achieved and how to duplicate success. The system can work for employees at all levels of the organization.

SOURCE: "Competency Models Develop Top Performance" by Richard Montier et al., *T + D Magazine* (July 2006).

opportunities for you to offer frequent feedback and monitor progress.

Whatever methods work best for your managerial style, acknowledge and assess your employees' performance regularly. You might hold weekly progress meetings with individual employees or teams, for example. You also could write e-mails responding to employees' ideas or commenting on their accomplishments. And, of course, you should use monthly, quarterly, and annual performance reviews as an opportunity

Red Flags ✕◆

TELLING THE TRUTH

Performance evaluations should be truthful but not harsh. Have you made any of these mistakes during an employee evaluation?

- Failed to provide specific feedback on what the employee could be doing better

- Omitted negative feedback from other people even though it might help the employee improve

- Criticized the employee's behavior or performance too harshly

- Neglected to give the employee time to prepare a written self-appraisal

to provide honest feedback. Employees generally respond best to positive reinforcement, of course, but constructive criticism can be effective as well. As long as feedback is conveyed positively, it is likely that it will be well received.

Documenting Interactions

Documenting your interactions with an employee in writing is important for a number

> "A review should not be used to send negative messages to employees about their potential growth."
>
> —Dennis L. DeMey,
> author of *25 Essential Lessons for Employee Management*

of reasons. First, this written record of discussions, disagreements, observations, and progress made toward goals is useful in conducting performance reviews.

Second, it provides a record of an employee's accomplishments and outstanding performance that may help to justify recognition, reward, or promotion.

Third, this documentation may be needed when a staff member has a dispute with you or the company, or you decide to terminate an employee.

Managers should keep a written account of employee interactions, recording both positive and negative events soon after they occur. Note the date and time, along with what you said and what the employee said, as you best recall it. Include the names of any witnesses to an event or other participants in a meeting. Document all interactions, conversations, and meetings with an employee, as well as all performance evaluations and disciplinary actions. Keep copies of any other information about an employee, whether positive or negative, formal or informal.

FORMAL REVIEWS

A standard procedure in evaluating an employee is the performance review, a formal meeting in which the manager tells employees how they are doing and what they can do better. Ideally, managers should meet with each employee at least quarterly. You should view this as a "developmental" meeting rather than an "appraisal": Your goal is to guide the employee toward success through your evaluation and feedback.

Evaluation

Some companies have performance appraisal forms with rating scales or checklists, while others permit a more narrative approach. Which format you use isn't as important as the information you convey to the employee and how you convey it.

Plan B

SELF-EVALUATION CAN BE REVEALING

Request that an employee submit a written self-evaluation before a performance evaluation. If you find that the employee's appraisal is generally similar to yours, then employee and employer expectations are probably being met.

If, however, this self-assessment is way off, you need to take action of some kind to align the employee's impressions with your observations. Average performers who rate themselves highly need a reality check— their self-inflated value needs to be brought down to Earth with some plain speaking on your part.

On the other hand, there are some outstanding employees who rate their performance as below average and are consistently too hard on themselves. They need repeated positive reinforcement and encouragement.

Self-evaluation is an opportunity to have a frank dialogue with an employee whose self-perception of performance doesn't match up with yours. This is a good way to reset expectations and motivate an employee at the same time.

If you have been providing frequent feedback and documenting your interactions with the employee, as suggested above, you will be in a much better position to conduct a thorough, comprehensive, and objective evaluation. Spend adequate time collecting, organizing, and summarizing your documentation. Incorporate this information onto the company's review form, or create your own form. Refer to the original job description, and use the job responsibilities as a checklist for rating the employee's performance.

In the review, include 360-degree feedback, confidentially collected from the employee's coworkers, vendors, customers, and other regular contacts. Their comments and experiences enrich the evaluation with an outside perspective. The result will be a more well-rounded and objective review.

Write the review in advance of the meeting. Consider asking the employee to submit a self-evaluation before the meeting as well. (Some companies encourage this concept and provide a self-review form to facilitate the process.) Compare the employee's self-evaluation with yours; the employee's perceptions may be considerably different. If so, this is a valuable springboard for discussion at the review meeting.

Feedback

Employees often dread their performance reviews, yet they can be a valuable experience (for you and your employee) if handled properly. An employee should not be intimidated by a performance evaluation—the whole experience

Dos & Don'ts ☑

PERFORMANCE REVIEWS

Make the most of performance reviews. Prepare for them, seek others' opinions about the employees being reviewed, keep the appointments on schedule, and involve your employees.

- ☐ Don't limit your performance evaluations to an annual appraisal.
- ☐ Do evaluate each employee's performance on at least a quarterly basis.
- ☐ Do make an effort to give informal feedback often.
- ☐ Don't miss opportunities to offer praise and encouragement.

should be nonthreatening and constructive. This is why it is essential for you to present feedback to the employee in a positive way.

In addition, consider how you can make the evaluation motivational. Always emphasize the employee's strengths and praise accomplishments. Address areas that need to be developed as well, but also offer employees a chance to collaborate on the process.

Hold the review meeting in a private place and schedule enough time so that you are not rushed. Go over your written evaluation right before the review so you can refer to it during the meeting without having to read it to the employee.

- ☐ Do get 360-degree feedback for a more thorough evaluation.
- ☐ Don't offer negative feedback without a constructive component.
- ☐ Don't discourage employees from sharing their thoughts and feelings during an evaluation.
- ☐ Don't delay or postpone a scheduled evaluation.
- ☐ Do view evaluations as part of a comprehensive performance management process.

Instead of giving the document to the employee right away as the meeting begins, start by reiterating the importance of performance reviews and then give an overview of the results. Highlight positive elements of the review first and, if appropriate, read selected portions of the document. Maintain eye contact and speak conversationally.

After highlighting the positives, move on to the negatives. Back these up with specific examples, excerpting quotes from the 360-degree feedback, if appropriate. Present the negatives as constructive criticism in a way that doesn't damage the employee's ego.

The BIG Picture

DON'T UNDER-EVALUATE

Some managers aren't hard enough on their direct reports when evaluating performance. They overlook negative behavior and poor performance to "spare the employee's feelings." They also fear that a negative appraisal might land them in court or ruin a workplace relationship. Managers who under-evaluate often claim that "nobody gets hurt" by their omissions. In fact, lenient evaluations do hurt. They hurt the supervisor, the employee, the employee's coworkers, and the organization as a whole: employees lose an opportunity to improve, the supervisor loses credibility, and the company loses productivity. Evaluating all performance honestly and fairly is critical to success.

SOURCE: *The Complete Guide to Performance Appraisal* by Dick Grote (American Management Association, 1996).

Then compare your review with the employee's self-review. Use this as an opportunity to listen to the employee's feedback. Finally, invite an open discussion of the performance review overall. The meeting will be most productive if it is a dialogue between you and your employee that includes an honest, nonconfrontational discussion of what each party can do to help the other.

During this conversation, review existing goals to determine the employee's effectiveness in meeting them and agree on new goals for the coming months. A follow-up meeting can define these new goals more specifically.

Follow the same process for quarterly and annual evaluations. If you provide informal feedback regularly, and formally evaluate performance at least quarterly, the annual performance appraisal will be easier for both you and the employee to manage—and far less intimidating.

After any performance review, employees should walk away with a clear understanding of what they are doing right as well as what areas they need to improve—without feeling inadequate about any shortcomings. Be sure the employee signs and returns a copy of the review form to you and keeps a copy.

PROMOTING EMPLOYEES

"Use your influence to ensure that promotions to positions of senior leadership affirm what your organization really stands for."

—Peter Drucker,
management guru and author (1909–2005)

Nothing highlights an employee's achievement more than a promotion. Promoting an employee should also make you feel good; after all, as the employee's manager, you contributed to the person's career advancement. Deciding who merits a promotion, and when, is a big responsibility.

Generally the deserving employee exceeds expectations in many ways: leadership ability, initiative, productivity, and diplomacy in dealing with coworkers and superiors.

A promotion isn't simply a change in job title. It should carry with it an increase in responsibility and authority, which may include managing employees, projects, resources, business initiatives, and budgets.

> "I have always felt that the most successful companies have a practice of promoting from within."
>
> David Packard,
> cofounder of Hewlett-Packard
> and author of *The HP Way*
> (1912–1996)

The traditional time to promote an employee is at the annual review, but a promotion can and should occur when it is most appropriate. The time may be right when the employee has been outstanding at supervising others, made exceptional contributions to a team's efforts, or exceeded goals. While promoting employees should be based on individual achievements, it is acceptable to time a promotion with a departmental reorganization, or when a position becomes available due to a resignation or termination.

Promoting a "Star"

It's always preferable to promote from within an organization. Some organizations make it a policy to review the qualifications of internal candidates first for any open position. Filling a position with a qualified internal candidate sends an important message to other employees that there is opportunity for advancement.

The BIG Picture

THE DESIRE TO MOVE UP

Today's managers are challenged by young people who want—and even expect—quick promotions. After a year or two at a job, younger workers are eager to move up. A manager must assess if the individual is ready for promotion and also if a legitimate higher-level spot exists.

In a competitive employment environment, younger workers' desire to move up may motivate them to leave one company prematurely for a higher-level position at another company. Older workers who have been in the workforce for a while generally have more realistic expectations.

If a managerial position opens up, evaluate the performance of your existing employees. An exceptional performer may be ready to take on a new challenge. If this person contributes to the team effort and is well liked by coworkers, the chances for a successful transition are even better. However, there is a potential pitfall to moving a "star" into a managerial position. Often, such a person has excelled as an individual contributor and has been recognized for independent achievement. As a manager, that same person will be expected to become a leader

Behind the Numbers

PROMOTE FROM WITHIN

Promoting from within can drive business performance upward. According to Michael Watkins, founder of Genesis Advisers LLC in West Newton, Massachusetts: "Forty percent of executives brought in from outside fail within 18 months; half will have left the company." In contrast, executives and managers promoted from within generally reach levels of peak performance more rapidly than outside recruits, and they're more likely to stick around.

SOURCE: "Developing Talent" by Robert J. Grossman, *HR Magazine* (January 2006).

of others, which requires a different mindset and, sometimes, a different skill set.

The star now needs to depend on others to be successful and must learn to delegate, to work collaboratively, to encourage others to be stars, and—what is hardest of all—to allow others to enjoy the limelight. At the same time, the star

PROMOTING TOO QUICKLY CAN BE HARMFUL

Promoting a young manager may seem like the right thing to do, but it could actually impede the manager's emotional development. Does the employee have the maturity to negotiate with peers, keep emotions under control during a crisis, and gain the support of others for important initiatives? The ability to persuade, influence, and work with all levels of management can be more important than ambition and talent. Delaying the promotion of junior managers until they have developed their people skills through time and experience might be more beneficial in the long run.

SOURCE: "The Young and the Clueless" by Kerry A. Bunker et al., *Harvard Business Review* On Point Enhanced Edition (December 1, 2002).

THE BOTTOM LINE

must accept the ultimate responsibility for the team's success or failure.

As the star's manager, you need to make it clear that this employee's criteria for success have changed. This can be an opportunity for you to

> "Nothing does more harm than the too common practice of . . . denying a good man promotion because 'we don't know what we'd do without him.' The promotion system must insure that everybody who is eligible is considered—and not just the most highly 'visible' people."
>
> —Peter Drucker

help a promising employee grow and develop. You can help the newly promoted employee set goals for the new position and also establish standards for performance management, so that the employee will be prepared in turn to evaluate the performance of others.

Dos & Don'ts ☑

HOW TO PROMOTE

Promoting an employee may be the right thing to do . . . but it should be done the right way.

☐ Do promote from within if possible.

☐ Don't use a promotion to reward an employee's one-time achievement.

☐ Do use a promotion as an opportunity to celebrate an employee's continuing efforts and hard work.

☐ Don't assume a "star" employee who is promoted will automatically be capable of working collaboratively with others.

☐ Do promote an individual who is ready to supervise others.

☐ Do make sure employees fully understand the responsibilities and authority that come with being promoted.

☐ Don't promote just to prevent a valued employee from resigning.

☐ Do be ready for a variety of reactions to a promotion, both positive and negative, from other employees.

Collaborative Promotions

Managers who believe their employees should have a say in the team's direction and makeup might try a new approach to promotions: encouraging employees to collaborate on them.

CASE *FILE*

PROMOTION OPPORTUNITIES MOTIVATE WORKERS

When workers are performing at lackluster levels, you might consider how the corporate climate is affecting them. According to a Watson Wyatt Worldwide study of 27 manufacturing sites, when employees feel that their work is meaningful, that they have support from fellow workers, and that the organization offers not only a solid performance management plan but also the opportunity for growth or promotion, their performance and productivity improves while absenteeism decreases. In particular, when workers feel there is an opportunity to be promoted for excellent, consistent performance, they tend to do their jobs well.

SOURCE: *Rewards and Business Strategy* by Howard C. Weizmann and Jane K. Weizmann (Watson Wyatt Worldwide, 2000).

The **BIG** Picture

THE CRITERIA FOR PROMOTION

A promotion is an employer's way of recognizing employees who have proven themselves worthy of increased responsibility. Employers should look at four key factors when deciding on promotions:

- **Job mastery** – Does the employee do the job well and with confidence?

- **Initiative** – Does the employee anticipate what needs to be done—and do it—without being told?

- **Work habits** – Does the employee have discipline and positive character traits?

- **Responsibility** – Can the employee handle complex decision-making and managerial obligations?

SOURCE: *Leadership, Personal Development and Career Success* by Cliff Ricketts (Thompson Delmar Learning, 2003).

You can invite employees to comment on the qualifications and job description for an open position. Then ask them to submit the names of candidates they feel would be suitable and include reasons for their choices; employees also can submit their own names, if appropriate.

This approach guarantees that all employees have a say in the promotion process. And that may make it easier for them to welcome the individual who ultimately gets the job.

Delivering the News about a Promotion

Promoting an employee is a celebratory experience. If handled correctly, the promotion can be as positive and motivational for coworkers—and for you as a manager—as it is for the employee.

The first person to tell about the promotion (after your supervisor) is the employee. You have the wonderful opportunity to give this person the good news. It is usually best conveyed first in a private meeting, followed by a public announcement to the individual's work group. It's a good idea to announce the promotion to all employees at the same time and hold a small celebration if you feel it's warranted.

An employee's promotion can be met by coworkers with both happiness and resentment. The promotion of a deserving employee may generate widespread approval, but this isn't always the case. Don't base your decision to promote someone on the anticipated reaction of coworkers, but be prepared for anything. Remember that you can't make everyone happy all the time. You can, however, work to help everyone understand and accept your decision. If you know there are other employees in the group who might be especially upset by the promotion—perhaps because they had expected to be chosen for the position—you might want to tell them about it privately, before announcing the

• POWER POINTS •

ANNOUNCING A PROMOTION

Telling individuals about a promotion at the right time makes a difference:

- Share the news and congratulations privately with the person who is being promoted first.

- Announce the promotion to your work group next. Tell everyone at the same time, unless you know someone in particular will object to the promotion. If that's the case, tell that employee privately, before informing the work group, and reinforce that individual's value to the organization.

- State the reasons for the promotion and make it a positive experience for the work group.

- Announce the promotion beyond the work group if appropriate.

- Document in writing your reasons and rationale for promoting the employee.

news to the group. Explain your reasons for the decision to them and reemphasize their value to the organization.

Be sure you document in writing the reasons and rationale for promoting an employee and keep this information on file.

A Learning Experience for All

An individual who is promoted should be symbolic of what it takes to achieve success in your organization. A promotion presents you with an opportunity to reinforce company values. It should be clear to promoted employees and

DEBUNKING PROMOTION MYTHS

Some widespread beliefs about being promoted are wrong, according to "The Realities of Management Promotion" by Marian N. Ruderman, a research report published by the Center for Creative Leadership:

People are promoted for their qualities – While initiative, persistence, dedication, and strong skills are important, politics can be critical. Managers must be comfortable with the people they promote and feel that they can trust them. Individuals who are politically wise will be promoted over those who aren't.

their coworkers that determination, initiative, and hard work pay off, and that individuals are rewarded for their superior efforts.

Every promotion should be a positive learning experience. The promoted employee learns new management skills, you learn how to mentor an emerging leader, and coworkers learn how to accept and work with a new manager.

The choice you make when you decide to promote, and how you handle the change when the promotion occurs, both with the individual and with the work group, will say a lot about you as a manager.

Promotions reward past performance – This is partially true, but promotions are also sometimes affected by circumstantial factors. For instance, someone's availability to relocate may be an important consideration in the decision to promote someone.

Outstanding performance reviews lead to promotions – Actually, bosses rely mostly on the opinion of others and their own gut feeling. They often ignore performance appraisals when deciding who should be promoted.

SOURCE: "Get Promoted Without Promoting Yourself" by Bill Breen, *Fast Company* (June 1996).

THE BOTTOM LINE

Alternatives to Promoting an Employee

While a promotion is often given to recognize effort and achievement, it may not always be the best action to take. Here are some instances when a promotion could potentially backfire:

Promoting to prevent a resignation. If a valuable employee expresses an intention to resign, your first instinct may be to offer a promotion to prevent it. However, under these conditions such an offer might compromise your organization by advancing an employee prematurely, establishing an unnecessary new position, or creating resentment among other employees.

Instead, first determine if the employee would consider staying if certain conditions were changed. Before you use promotion as a retention strategy, try to find out what the employee

• POWER POINTS •

PROMOTING FOR THE RIGHT REASONS

Promote an employee who consistently demonstrates these qualities:

- Leadership ability
- Sustained excellence
- Success at meeting goals
- High productivity
- Initiative
- Diplomacy in dealing with others

really wants: better working conditions, a more flexible schedule, increased compensation?

CASE *FILE*

ACT YOUR AGE

Susan, a client of executive coach Lois B. Frankel, was stuck in a midlevel position despite the fact that she was well liked and did her job competently.

Frankel realized that to get along with everyone at work, Susan displayed a niceness that came across as naivete. Although people liked Susan, they didn't believe she was mature enough to receive more responsibilities and to be promoted.

If you're looking for a promotion, it's critical to project the right image and to be aware of the impression you are making on those who have decision-making power over your career. If you are in charge of managing and promoting others, take to heart the old saying "don't judge a book by its cover." Instead, get to know your employees well, observe their behavior, evaluate their capabilities, and ask lots of questions about their career ambitions. Looks (and sometimes behavior) might be deceiving.

SOURCE: *Nice Girls Don't Get the Corner Office* by Lois B. Frankel (Warner Books, 2004).

CASE FILE

THE LAST PERSON YOU'D PROMOTE

Big Bill was a hard-boiled union technician for a Fortune 500 entertainment company. Management was generally afraid to deal with him directly because of his tough and adversarial attitude. One manager, however, who had noted how skilled Big Bill was at designing lighting for shows, was able to convince his superiors that Big Bill should be given a shot at supervising the lighting crews. After being promoted, Bill became one of the most respected players on the technical design team. Like anyone else, Bill hadn't appreciated being ignored and marginalized. He just reacted with more vitriol than the average person. Once he was recognized for his talent, he won the respect of many former adversaries. The promotion paid enormous dividends for the company.

SOURCE: *How to Work for an Idiot* by John Hoover (Career Press, 2003).

Some of these things may be easier to provide and have less of an impact on the organization than a promotion.

Promoting to recognize exceptional one-time performance. Sometimes an employee will do something truly exceptional. A salesperson may have a tremendous month in a new business, an employee in the financial department may work several weekends to close the books, or an ambitious worker may write and present a report that impresses a manager's superiors. Such one-time efforts that go above and beyond normal performance should not be overlooked. At the very least, the manager should recognize the employee's exceptional efforts with a personal thank-you, public congratulations, or a spot bonus.

A promotion, however, should not be a reward for one-time performance—it is the organization's recognition that an individual is ready to advance to the next supervisory or management level. A promotion is earned by sustained effort over time and should fill a position that already exists or one that can be created appropriately.

Promoting to maintain organizational parity. In large organizations, managers tend to become protective of their department or division. One way to maintain organizational stature is to keep increasing a department's size and importance through promotions. Even if they are not justified, a manager may push for them just to keep up with other department heads.

Typically, such promotions are ill-founded. If the employees who have been promoted are not ready for advancement, the manager will soon recognize their inadequacies, and other employees in the department will deride the promotion. In the long run, this type of organizational game benefits no one.

DEALING WITH UNDERPERFORMERS

"The only way to deliver to the people who are achieving is not to burden them with the people who are not achieving."

—Jim Collins,
author of *Good to Great*

Inevitably, a small percentage of your employees will be underperformers: they will do only the minimum to get by, they will fail to meet your expectations, or they will be troublesome to your organization. This is a reality virtually every organization and manager faces.

THE PROBLEM OF UNDERPERFORMERS

Once you identify an underperformer, it is your job either to rectify the situation or to move the individual out of the organization.

When you observe an employee underperforming or doing something wrong, act promptly. It is equally important to address the issue alone with the employee, not in front of others. If a coworker brings another employee's sub-par performance or misdeed to your attention, you still need to act, but do so with care. Try to corroborate the story, and be tactful in confronting the employee with secondhand information.

When dealing with any performance or disciplinary issue, it is important to maintain your objectivity. Give the employee the benefit of the doubt. If your work environment has been one of mutual trust and respect from the start, you will be better prepared to deal with any problem that comes along.

Performance Problems Caused by Personal Issues

You can't allow an employee with performance problems caused by personal issues to undermine coworkers or disrupt the work environment. Yet when employees spend 40 hours or more per week at a job, disruptive personal issues are bound to overlap work time—it could be personality conflicts with coworkers, financial problems, childcare issues, marital discord, imbalance between work and life, substance abuse, or any other difficulty. Such problems distract employees from their work. The result may be increased absenteeism, many partial days off, an inability to concentrate, unmet deadlines, and so on. Depending on the nature of the problem, some work schedule flexibility may help—a temporary reduction in hours or some time off, if necessary.

If the issue is personal, your best course may be simply to listen and empathize, but not to attempt to solve the problem. Rather than give advice, help your employees talk through the

Red Flags ✎◆

ANTICIPATING DISCIPLINARY ISSUES

Noticeable alterations in an employee's behavior could signal a looming performance or disciplinary issue. Watch for:

- **Change in attitude** – A previously positive employee becomes negative and uncooperative.

- **Minimal effort** – An employee does just enough to get by but doesn't make any extra effort.

- **Lack of concentration** – An employee seems distracted or preoccupied.

- **The silent treatment** – An employee keeps to himself more than usual.

problem and arrive at their own solutions. If appropriate, advise the employee to seek professional counsel.

If the issue is directly related to the employee's position, you may be able to resolve it. If a coworker is involved, you may need to bring the two parties together to reach a compromise. Maintain your objectivity and encourage the employee with the problem to suggest solutions.

If an employee's poor performance has no obvious extenuating circumstances, you will need to address problems as they occur, as well as during performance reviews. Work with the employee to set specific goals for improvement, and monitor progress. If you don't see noticeable improvement, then remedial action, demotion, or termination may be necessary.

Performance Problems Due to a Bad Fit

Sometimes employees perform poorly because they are simply ill-suited for the position. Even if you followed the right hiring procedures, a person may not turn out to be a good fit for the job, your work group, or the company.

Such a problem can manifest itself in many ways: the employee's failure to meet basic job requirements, arguments with coworkers, or unexplained sick days. The individual may be visibly uncomfortable or seem out of place in the work environment, or act withdrawn.

If you suspect a performance problem is the result of a bad fit, hold a private meeting with the employee as soon as possible. Broach the issue honestly but diplomatically. Chances are the employee will feel relieved and want to talk about it, because being wrong for the job is as unsettling to the employee as it is for a manager. If no other suitable jobs exist within your group, determine through your human resources department what other positions might be available for the employee. Work out a plan to move

CASE *FILE*

A BAD FIT

Pamela Gingold, a bank manager, had to give an employee a poor review. The employee was a corporate finance analyst, but Gingold didn't think the woman was suited for the job. It seemed as if she wasn't serious about improving her skills. She clearly was more of a relationship-oriented person, who liked talking on the phone instead of doing financial analysis.

When Gingold discussed her concerns with the employee at the review, the woman took the advice to heart. Instead of getting defensive, she admitted to Gingold that she thought the job was a bad fit. The employee began a search, eventually moving out of the financial analyst position and into human resources at the bank.

SOURCE: "Review Went Badly? Stay Cool, Find a Fix or Look to Move On" by Erin White, *Wall Street Journal* (May 23, 2006).

the individual immediately. If no positions exist, consider terminating the employee and provide a generous severance.

Plan B

PRAISE THE WORK, NOT THE EMPLOYEE

When helping employees turn around performance, consider the power of praise. Letting them know they are doing a good job is often enough to motivate and maintain improved performance. But when giving praise, be aware that some people have problems accepting compliments and might push back.

It's always safe to express how pleased you are with the work the employee has done—for example, an increase in sales or production numbers, a decrease in customer complaints, or an on-schedule and under-budget project. Employees will feel energized that their efforts contributed to the success of the work being praised and that you acknowledged their good work. You'll get the positive effect of recognition without running the risk of embarrassing the employee.

SOURCE: *Workplace Investigations* by Donald W. Slowik (Evergreen Press, 1997).

WHAT TO DO ABOUT PERFORMANCE PROBLEMS

Recognizing that an employee is underperforming is one thing, trying to rectify the situation is quite another. Depending on the manager, confronting an underperforming employee can range from an unpleasant task to a management crisis. No one likes conflict in the workplace, and yet a responsible manager can't let a performance problem go unacknowledged.

Your first objective should be to improve the employee's behavior, if at all possible. Your company has made an investment in the employee, and, as a manager, you are better off getting an existing employee to meet performance standards than having to go through the recruitment and hiring process to refill the position. Sometimes, however, remediation simply doesn't work and you will be faced with the unpleasant task of demoting or even terminating an employee.

> "It isn't the people you fire who make your life miserable. It's the people you don't."
>
> —Harvey B. Mackay,
> author of *Swim with the Sharks without Being Eaten Alive*

Coaching

Providing frequent feedback and helping an employee move in the right direction is a good start toward remediation. For a serious performance problem, however, you need to escalate the feedback process and turn it into coaching.

Coaching involves a time commitment on your part. You will need to identify and help the employee improve his weakest performance areas, either through your own hands-on efforts or with specialized training. You may have to guide the employee by setting shorter-term goals, monitoring progress more closely, and scrutinizing the employee's work.

> "When you confront a problem, you begin to solve it."
>
> —Rudy Giuliani,
> former mayor of New York City

Though you personally can and should help the employee improve, three other approaches can distribute some of the burden:

Enlist the help of another employee in peer coaching. This person takes on the responsibility of coaching the underperforming employee and is offered an incentive for succeeding.

This is a win-win situation if the deficient employee's performance improves and the coach has the satisfaction of helping a peer.

CASE *FILE*

FINANCIAL FIRM USES PEER COACHING TO REDUCE EMPLOYEE TURNOVER

To battle a high employee turnover rate, WFS Financial, one of the nation's largest independent auto finance companies, instituted a peer-coaching program. At its regional collection center in Dallas, loan counselors were randomly assigned to "Talent Teams" of three employees each. Employees were also encouraged to conduct their own "equity reviews," in which the employees analyzed and considered the investment of time and experience they had made in their jobs and what they had received in return from the company. The Talent Teams met monthly for three months. Team members listened to each other, exchanged ideas, and helped each other solve problems. The program directly contributed to a reduction in employee turnover from about 33 percent to 21 percent.

SOURCE: "Peer Coaching Helps WFS Financial Curb Turnover" by Todd Henneman, *Workforce Management Online* (February 2005).

Ask your human resources department for help with volunteer peer coaches from other work groups, suggestions for training programs, or one-on-one assistance to the underperformer.

Sometimes "tough love" can work with an underperforming employee. A job in jeopardy can be a strong incentive for self-remediation. Work out an action plan with the employee that includes tightly defined improvement goals, and see if the person can rise to the occasion.

Progressive Discipline

Some people don't improve, even with coaching, in which case you may have to escalate your efforts with progressive discipline. Though usually associated with misconduct or negligence, discipline also may work for serious performance problems.

Managers who have good relationships with their employees will find it easier, not harder, to exercise discipline. Responsible employees who have received frequent informal feedback about their performance from a manager should be capable of making a correction without a big fuss. In effect, an empowered employee is a self-disciplined one.

If you feel you have no other option but to take disciplinary action, it should be meted out progressively or cumulatively. Employees should be aware of the behavior expected of them and of company rules and regulations.

If you have been giving feedback and evaluating your employees' performance regularly, few reprimands should be necessary. They should be issued only for just cause: misconduct, negligence, insubordination, unwillingness to perform job requirements, or similar circumstances. Some guidelines follow for delivering a reprimand.

The oral reprimand. If constructive criticism delivered in a private meeting fails to correct unacceptable behavior, a more official oral reprimand may be warranted. This is the first step in a progressive discipline process that may ultimately, but not necessarily, lead to termination.

> "Executives owe it to the organization and to their fellow workers not to tolerate nonperforming individuals in important jobs."
>
> —Peter Drucker

An oral reprimand means that you and your employee discuss a specific problem, and you call for an action to correct it. Explain the significance of an oral reprimand, the specific reasons for it, and how a more serious consequence could result if the employee doesn't take action promptly. Document the oral reprimand with a note in the employee's file.

The written reprimand. If the problem continues, you may need a more formal disciplinary action. A written reprimand, the next step, formally puts the employee on notice. You must ask the employee to acknowledge the written reprimand by signing and dating a copy, and you should file a copy with your human resources department. If the employee refuses to sign the reprimand, note this on your copy of the document, and on the human resources copy.

Reprimand protocols. Deliver both oral and written reprimands in private, and always give the employee an opportunity to respond verbally or in writing. Include specific references to the unacceptable behavior. Thoroughly document the nature of the action, when it occurred, and how it veered from acceptable standards.

Reprimanding an employee doesn't require you to be angry or upset. Maintain a calm demeanor even if the employee becomes emotional. Be firm yet fair in explaining the nature of the reprimand, and make it clear that additional disciplinary action could be taken if the problem isn't corrected.

Reprimanding an employee is never pleasant. Don't let that deter you, however, from acting promptly when necessary.

Demotions Because of Performance Issues

If an employee isn't performing up to department standards or can't handle the responsibilities of a particular position, a demotion or a transfer may be warranted. A demotion is the reduction of an employee's job responsibilities—and often compensation. If you have coached an underperforming employee and issued reprimands without seeing any improvement, then a demotion should come as no surprise. Still, it will be a blow to the person's ego.

Before you decide on demoting someone, get unbiased opinions in confidence from other

The BIG Picture

ARE DEMOTIONS NECESSARY?

In a well-managed organization, demotions should rarely be necessary.

Thorough job descriptions with clear statements of responsibilities and qualifications should result in the recruitment and hiring of the right people. An employee given the right amount of responsibility and supervision should be able to meet the challenges of the job. A good manager will help guide each person to succeed, so performance issues that could lead to a demotion should not arise.

Also, a well-run company is likely to have few reorganizations or layoffs, reducing the need for business-based demotions.

Outside the Box

A BLESSING IN DISGUISE

The story is told that when Winston Churchill was turned out of office after World War II, his wife consoled him by calling the ouster "a blessing in disguise." "If it is," said Churchill, "then it is very effectively disguised." As you contemplate the need to end your relationship with an employee, remember that somewhere out there, that individual will find a place where his or her skills and experience will be a perfect fit. Then think what Ronald Reagan achieved after being released by Warner Brothers and what Lee Iacocca accomplished after Henry Ford showed him the door.

SOURCE: *Swim with the Sharks Without Being Eaten Alive* by Harvey B. Mackay (HarperCollins, 1988).

managers, coworkers, and the human resources department. Be sure you have written documentation to support your decision.

Informing the employee of a demotion is an unpleasant but necessary task. Arrange a private meeting in your office. Build your case by briefly reviewing all unsuccessful efforts to improve the employee's performance. Calmly explain what the demotion means, why it is necessary, and when it will start.

Make it clear that there is still a place in the organization where the employee can contribute. Prepare a written document with the new job title, responsibilities, and revised compensation, and ask the employee to sign it and return a copy to you. Allow the employee the time to express any reactions. Acknowledge the person's feelings,

• POWER POINTS •

TERMINATING AN EMPLOYEE

Terminations are always difficult, even when they are clearly necessary. These points are worth remembering.

- Termination may be especially traumatic for junior employees because it could be their first experience of losing a job.

- Midlevel employees might be qualified for lateral transfers.

- Terminations of senior executives affect the whole organization.

- When senior people are terminated, other employees want to know how they will be affected.

- Severance pay should always be commensurate with the individual's years of service.

but maintain your position and reiterate the reasons that you arrived at your decision.

Terminating Employment of Underperformers

The last resort for dealing with an underperforming employee is termination. Before you consider this option, you should have offered

FIRING

According to former General Electric CEO Jack Welch, there are three ways that managers go wrong when firing people: They go about it too quickly, they are not truthful enough, or they delay doing it. A friend of his who had been promoted within a collegial, privately held company made the first mistake when she dismissed one of her direct reports rather suddenly. He had challenged her authority, repeatedly made negative comments, and missed deadlines—and didn't change his behavior when spoken to. When dismissed, he blew up, convened a meeting of his staff, and launched a "hate-management movement" that took about three months to die down.

SOURCE: *Winning* by Jack Welch (Collins, 2005).

THE BOTTOM LINE

the employee every opportunity to improve. Typically, you will have gone through the stages of coaching, discipline, and sometimes even demotion, all without seeing any significant improvement.

If you are convinced termination is inevitable, start the process by considering the exit strategy. As soon as you inform the employee of the termination, you will have another problem—the employee's job responsibilities. Think about

Behind the Numbers

TERMINATIONS THROUGH LAYOFFS

The Bureau of Labor Statistics did not start reporting layoffs—under the label "worker displacement"—until 1984. By 2004, the Bureau had reported that at least 30 million full-time workers had been permanently displaced. This number did not include the millions more who had been forced into early retirement, or those who had lost their jobs through some other form of downsizing that was not reported. More realistically, 7 or 8 percent, on average, of the nation's full-time workers have probably been laid off each year—nearly double the rate of recognized layoffs.

SOURCE: *The Disposable American* by Louis Uchitelle (Knopf, 2006).

how you will fill the hole before a replacement is recruited. How will you redistribute the work? Who is available to help you accomplish the work that will need to get done?

Then prepare for the termination itself. Good written documentation of past unresolved problems is essential. Review your records of your efforts with the employee and their unsatisfactory results to be certain you have justifiable reasons for termination. Be sure you know your

• POWER POINTS •

THE LIABILITY OF TERMINATION

When you terminate an employee, be sure to follow your organization's procedures and policies carefully and to comply with employment laws and regulations.

- Keep good written records and thoroughly document the reasons for termination.

- Never indicate, suggest, or imply that a termination is related to age, gender, or race.

- Issue a termination letter and have the employee sign a copy.

- For senior executives, execute a termination agreement and release.

company's policy on the matter, as well as the provisions of federal and state laws relating to termination.

Deliver the news to the employee calmly at a private meeting in your office or in the human resources department, preferably with a representative there. Present a letter to the employee with a termination date and the details of any severance package or other benefits.

An employee's reaction can range from resigned acceptance to dejection to disbelief to anger to tears. Show compassion, but be firm

The BIG Picture

BEING A COUNSELOR

An employee who is terminated can go through many emotional stages—denial, anger, despair, fear, and, eventually, acceptance.

Junior employees who have never lost a job might feel particularly vulnerable. A manager faced with terminating a junior employee should be prepared to offer some counsel.

Explain that joblessness will be temporary, that many people lose jobs, and that another job will be found. Do your best to help the employee maintain self-confidence. Offer referrals to other potential hiring managers of your acquaintance, if appropriate.

and make it clear that the decision is final. Your objective is to terminate the employee without compromising anyone's dignity.

Terminating Junior Employees

Most employers use an "at-will" employment policy, which essentially means the employer can terminate a worker at any time for any legal reason.

Additionally, many employers offer new employees positions on a probationary basis, which specifies a period of time, typically

WORKING TOGETHER AFTER EMPLOYMENT ENDS

If a senior-level employee is terminated for reasons other than poor performance, a relationship with the company can be maintained and is often mutually beneficial. By contracting with the individual on an hourly basis, the company can benefit from a former senior employee's experience without incurring direct overhead costs. Former senior employees are often so familiar with the company's processes that they are highly efficient even when working outside the organization.

From the individual's perspective, a part-time consulting relationship may be an attractive alternative to a full-time job.

90 days, within which the employer can terminate the new employee without cause.

Although subject to state and federal laws, both of these policies generally protect an employer's right to terminate employment at any time. Such policies, however, should not replace a well-documented termination process.

Many managers think that it is easier to terminate junior employees, because they are entry-level or hold less important positions. Termination may be especially traumatic for them, however, because it may be their first job

Plan B

An executive's termination usually involves an agreement that provides the employee with a severance package and, in return, assures that no legal action will be pursued against the employer.

If the individual is over 40, the Age Discrimination in Employment Act (ADEA) may be relevant. Under ADEA, your organization might consider offering the terminated employee a Voluntary Early Retirement Program (VERP). The Older Workers Benefits Protection Act (OWBPA) provides specific requirements for obtaining a release from an employee over 40.

Dos & Don'ts ☑

TERMINATION

Terminating an employee is the most dreaded management task. Follow these suggestions for handling performance-based termination with respect for the employee and with professionalism.

☐ Do provide periodic feedback and regular performance evaluations to prevent the need for termination.

☐ Do consider alternatives to termination, such as demotions or transfers.

☐ Don't terminate an employee without fully documenting your reasons.

or first experience with losing a job. Consider alternatives to termination, such as demotions or lateral transfers. If termination is inevitable, thoroughly document the reasons for the termination and follow your organization's policies.

Terminating Midlevel Employees

Your organization's investment in midlevel employees is higher than for junior employees. Midlevel employees not only receive higher compensation, they also tend to be older, which results in higher costs associated with health, life, and disability insurance packages. If you have been monitoring performance and doing

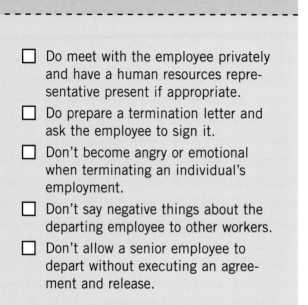

☐ Do meet with the employee privately and have a human resources representative present if appropriate.

☐ Do prepare a termination letter and ask the employee to sign it.

☐ Don't become angry or emotional when terminating an individual's employment.

☐ Don't say negative things about the departing employee to other workers.

☐ Don't allow a senior employee to depart without executing an agreement and release.

periodic performance evaluations, the reason for terminating a midlevel employee is less likely to be poor performance and more likely to follow a reorganization or period of layoffs. Consider alternatives such as lateral transfers. Because a midlevel employee may have skills that are applicable in other parts of your organization, a transfer to another facility or even a different region might be an option.

For midlevel employees, offering severance pay commensurate with years of service, referrals to other potential employers, and assistance from the company's employment recruiters are appropriate. Give the terminated employee some time

WORK**FLOW** TOOLS

PROGRESSIVE DISCIPLINE STEPS

INFORMAL FEEDBACK
Given during and after
projects and tasks and
always documented in writing

PERFORMANCE REVIEWS
Given quarterly and annually

ORAL REPRIMANDS
Always given in private

WRITTEN REPRIMANDS
To be signed by employee

PROBATION
Final warning

TERMINATION
The last resort

to adjust to the news. Then ask how coworkers should be informed and respect the employee's wishes. Some terminated midlevel employees want to tell coworkers themselves; others prefer that the announcement come from you. Don't discourage good-bye parties, but don't be surprised if you are not invited.

Terminating Senior Employees

Two issues are of primary concern when a senior employee must be terminated—the impact on the organization and the financial details. Any senior-level termination will be disruptive to your organization. The departure may be perceived as the harbinger of a major reorganization, a sign that the company is in trouble, a warning of layoffs ahead, or the like.

Therefore, careful management of the termination process is crucial. Once the other executives have been told, senior management should inform all the organization's employees at the same time. Tell employees as much as they need to know to assure them that the change isn't indicative of a deeper problem in the company.

Other regulations covered by such laws as the Employee Retirement Income Security Act (ERISA) and the Consolidated Omnibus Budget Reconciliation Act (COBRA) apply to senior-level employees. Review all applicable laws carefully before reaching any final agreement.

The best-case scenario is for the organization and the executive to reach common ground and work out satisfactory terms, and then for the individual to depart without major disruption.

EVALUATING TEAM PERFORMANCE

"Groups become great only when everyone in them, leaders and members alike, is free to do his or her absolute best."

—Warren Bennis and Patricia Ward Biederman, authors of *Organizing Genius*

Evaluating the performance of a team is different from evaluating the performance of an individual employee. In general, however, applying the basic strategies outlined in previous chapters to groups of employees will help you evaluate and manage team performance effectively.

Self-Assessment Quiz

CAN YOU EVALUATE AND MANAGE TEAM PERFORMANCE?

Read each of the following statements and indicate whether you agree or disagree. Then check your score at the end.

1. I set high standards for performance.

   ○ Agree   ○ Disagree

2. I convey a sense of common purpose and direction to my team.

   ○ Agree   ○ Disagree

3. I recruit individuals with specific skills to help the team succeed.

   ○ Agree   ○ Disagree

4. I establish a few immediate performance-oriented goals for the team.

   ○ Agree   ○ Disagree

5. I monitor the team's performance and hold regular progress meetings.

   ○ Agree   ○ Disagree

6. I identify the weakest members of the team and try to find ways to help them improve their performance.

   ○ Agree   ○ Disagree

7. I help the team establish checkpoints to track performance.

   ○ Agree   ○ Disagree

8. If I see my team underperforming, I analyze the possible reasons and address them immediately.

    O Agree   O Disagree

9. If my team becomes dysfunctional, I redirect them.

    O Agree   O Disagree

10. I recognize that a team member's changing role can affect the team's overall performance.

    O Agree   O Disagree

Scoring
Give yourself 1 point for every question you answered "Agree" and 0 points for every question you answered "Disagree."

Analysis

8–10   You can effectively evaluate and manage team performance.

5–7   You need some work on your team performance management skills.

0–4   You need to improve significantly if you want to effectively manage team performance.

Be aware, however, that managing a team's performance is more challenging and complex than one-on-one performance management.

As you will see, you need to apply your management skills to interpersonal relationships,

> "Winning leaders make their goals seem attainable by building up the players' confidence and determination. One of the best ways to do that is by acknowledging the difficulties and creating 'we're all in this together' teamwork. Where single individuals may despair of accomplishing a monumental task, teams nurture, support and inspire each other."
>
> —Noel Tichy,
> author of *The Leadership Engine*

team dynamics, and performance issues that affect the group as a whole, rather than just a single individual.

What do you do, for example, when some team members seem to be working toward different objectives, or when one or two team members are clearly out-performing others? How do you keep team members of varying

Behind the Numbers

PERFORMANCE LOSS IN TEAMS

Research conducted by Michael C. Mankins and Richard Steele suggests that the average team achieves only 63 percent of the objectives of their strategic plans. A survey of business managers at large companies indicated that teams experienced an average 37 percent "performance loss." In rating various aspects of the planning and execution process, managers said the top three reasons for performance loss were, in order of importance, inadequate or unavailable resources, a poorly communicated strategy, and the failure to define the actions required to execute the strategy.

SOURCE: "Turning Strategy into Great Performance" by Michael C. Mankins and Richard Steele, *Harvard Business Review* (August 2005).

ability performing on an equal level? What do you do when an underperforming team member affects the morale of the others? Once you can answer these questions and act on them, you'll be better equipped to manage—and to evaluate—team performance.

HOW TO EVALUATE TEAMS

When you build a team, you bring together people of varying capabilities, personalities, and work styles and form them into one cohesive unit. Ideally, each individual brings a skill set in a particular area that combines with those of

Red Flags ✗◆

TEAM PERFORMANCE KILLERS

Three common "megatraps" can kill team performance, says corporate survival expert Steven R. Rayner:

The strategic blunder – Organizations fall prey to market conditions, competitive threats, or technological change. Even a great internal management structure may not help a company succeed. Team performance will suffer when the company makes strategic blunders.

The collision of cultures – Changes to a team's charter and membership, which are common during a consolidation, will sometimes destroy a team's effectiveness.

other members to create an effective team. Getting individual team members to work together is one thing—ensuring that they perform well as a single unit is another.

To manage and evaluate a team's performance, start by setting performance standards and goals that every member can understand and embrace. As a manager and team leader, you need to communicate to team members what their mission is, how you expect them to accomplish it, the challenges you anticipate along the way, and how you will measure the team's success. You need to foster collaboration and cooperation and at the

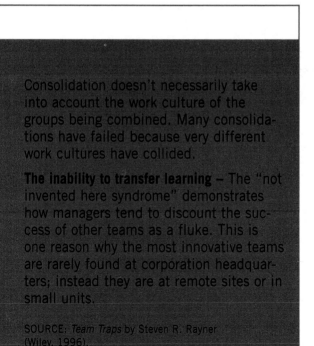

Consolidation doesn't necessarily take into account the work culture of the groups being combined. Many consolidations have failed because very different work cultures have collided.

The inability to transfer learning – The "not invented here syndrome" demonstrates how managers tend to discount the success of other teams as a fluke. This is one reason why the most innovative teams are rarely found at corporation headquarters; instead they are at remote sites or in small units.

SOURCE: *Team Traps* by Steven R. Rayner (Wiley, 1996).

same time take the initiative in solving problems, meeting deadlines for deliverables, focusing on the team's goals, achieving maximum productivity, and striving for overall excellence.

> "A common set of demanding performance goals that a group considers important to achieve will lead, most of the time, to both performance and a team. Performance, however, is the primary objective while a team remains the means, not the end."
>
> —Jon R. Katzenbach and Douglas K. Smith, authors of *The Wisdom of Teams*

Measuring Team Progress with Goals

Goal setting for teams is somewhat different from goal setting for individuals. The manager's first responsibility is to convey to the team a sense of common purpose and direction. Define the team's specific responsibilities and explain how the team's work supports the larger organization's goals. Because teams have a single driving purpose, sometimes the perspective of individual members can become too narrow and focused on one thing. Although this is helpful in getting the work accomplished, it also means that team members can lose sight of the bigger picture. Remind them of the value of their efforts beyond the confines of the team. How is the team contributing to the greater good?

Outside the Box

VIRTUOSO TEAMS

When big changes and high performance levels are required, consider forming a "virtuoso team," composed of people with expertise in specific fields. These teams are formed for particularly challenging projects and tend to work with high energy.

One of the challenges of managing a virtuoso team is getting such top talent to work together effectively. But if a manager can marshal these forces, virtuoso teams can accomplish remarkable things that can revolutionize businesses, and even entire industries.

SOURCE: "Virtuoso Teams" by Bill Fischer and Andy Boynton, *Harvard Business Review* (July/August 2005).

Set goals that are specific and measurable, with deliverables and due dates, and encourage team accountability. Ask this basic question in creating an effective goal: Exactly what does the team need to deliver, in what quantity, and by what date? As Katzenbach and Smith recommend in their book *The Wisdom of Teams,* establish a few immediate performance-oriented tasks and goals, and challenge the team regularly with fresh facts and information.

Allow all team members to help set the goals. Build consensus early so everyone feels a sense of

CASE *FILE*

TRAINING WITH FRIES

In the spring of 2003, McDonald's was experiencing disappointing business performance. To turn the situation around, the company embarked on a new program of training and performance measurement for its 1.6 million employees called "The Plan to Win." Central to this program was a consistent emphasis on measurement and accountability throughout the company.

Employees from up to 20 surrounding McDonald's restaurants would gather at a "seed store" for hands-on training, then return to their restaurants to train their teams. McDonald's would measure the success of their training in part by

common purpose and collective ownership. Your team members need to see the value of working together and to take pride in the result of their collaborative efforts.

Typically, a single goal will involve the collaborative efforts of all team members. However, certain team members may need to take individual responsibility for specific portions of the work because of their unique skills. They should keep other team members informed, however; this "be aware and share" attitude is essential to an effective team.

Once the team understands and embraces the goals, help them establish benchmarks

how fast the employees rolled out a customer order and by the rate of employee turnover at each restaurant. Team performance was also measured by key factors such as how accurately the team processed an order, getting the right ingredients, portioning, temperature, etc. According to Ralph Alvarez, President and COO of McDonald's, "When we short-cut training, we see it in lack of performance of products."

As McDonald's efforts demonstrate, team training and performance management go hand in hand.

SOURCE: "Training: They're Loving It" by Barry Bingham and Pat Galagan, *T + D Magazine* (November 2006).

for meeting these goals to measure progress along the way. These benchmarks may be based on the experience of other teams in the organization, or they may be set in a team meeting. Appoint a team member to post the

CASE *FILE*

TEAMS WHO CONNECT TO THEIR CUSTOMERS

Production workers at Super Sack Manufacturing Corporation in Texas are organized into self-directed work teams that are not only dedicated to specific customers but authorized to communicate directly with them.

By getting to know their customers better, they become familiar with their unique requirements. By being given permission to solve the customer's problems, the production team can make specific improvements to its performance on behalf of that customer. The company's director of quality says customers are surprised and impressed when they receive letters from a production team. Many of the letters include suggestions that result in cost savings for the customer.

SOURCE: *301 Great Customer Service Ideas* by Nancy Artz (Inc. Publishing, 1997).

benchmarks on a calendar or in a project-management software program.

Benchmarks are checkpoints. Since their purpose is to measure your rate of progress, they should be reviewed regularly. As the team leader, you should schedule progress meetings weekly or monthly, depending on the intensity of the work schedule.

• POWER POINTS •

PROGRESS AND GOALS

Set goals for your team and monitor their progress:

- Convey a sense of common purpose and direction.

- Explain how the team's work supports the larger organization's goals.

- Set specific, measurable goals and encourage team accountability.

- Help the team establish benchmarks or checkpoints to measure the rate of their progress.

- Hold regular progress meetings for the entire team to report on the benchmarks reached so far.

- Use successful completion of goals to evaluate and manage team performance.

Individual team members and smaller working groups should report to the entire team on their progress toward meeting the benchmarks, which

MOTIVATING A TEAM TO IMPROVE PERFORMANCE

In *Reinventing Leadership,* Warren Bennis and Robert Townsend emphasize the importance of keeping your staff highly motivated. You want to enhance the ability of your team to work together and achieve higher levels of performance. They suggest you ask yourself these questions about your team:

- Are my people excited?

- Are they energetic?

- Are they creative?

- Are they free to make mistakes?

- If not, what's chaining them?

- What in the organization can I get rid of that will free them to be as creative and energetic and excited as they can be?

SOURCE: *Reinventing Leadership* by Warren Bennis and Robert Townsend (Morrow, 1995).

THE BOTTOM LINE

keeps everyone up to date and helps you assess whether the team's work is on track.

Use the goals you set as a checklist to evaluate overall team performance. If you see that progress is slipping, you need to work with your team members to try to identify problem areas. You can choose to revise your goals—particularly if

Dos & Don'ts ☑

TEAM MEMBERS' PERFORMANCE

Managing a team's performance is essential—but so is managing and evaluating individual team members.

- ☐ Do recognize the strengths and weaknesses of each team member.

- ☐ Do understand who might be best suited to different roles on the team.

- ☐ Do identify the weakest links of a team and help them improve their deficiencies.

- ☐ Don't assume every team member shares the same commitment to the team and will work as hard as other team members.

- ☐ Do meet with the members you perceive to be team leaders and get their opinions on other team members.

the problems are beyond the team's control—but you should do so only when you have a very compelling reason.

CASE *FILE*

A TEAM DESIGNED FOR HIGH PERFORMANCE

Bobby Braun was the project leader for a NASA team that in 2003 built a space capsule designed to bring samples from Mars back to Earth. The "Mars Sample Return Mission" was part of NASA's initiative to achieve faster results with smaller teams. The team performed risk analyses to find potential problems. But sometimes, assistant project manager Lisa Simonson said, gut feelings led to decisions. "We have confidence in each other and in the process," said Simonson. Braun confirmed that the team's shared confidence and mutual respect enabled them to make decisions efficiently and with a minimum of internal disagreements. By having a unified goal and focus, this team achieved outstanding performance.

SOURCE: "Xtreme Teams" by Cheryl Dahle, *Fast Company* (November 1999).

Evaluating the Performance of Each Member of the Team

Not all team members are equally competent. Get to know the strengths and weaknesses of your individual team members. Recognize that some team members may be better suited to certain tasks than others. Part of your success as a team leader is to understand who will be the best for different roles on the team. Putting the right people in the right roles can strengthen overall performance.

Some individuals on the team may require training to reach the standards you have set. Provide on-the-job and outside training as required. If necessary, get stronger team members to supervise or assist weaker ones. It is your job to identify the team's weakest links and help them improve their deficiencies. If you don't, the entire team will suffer.

Also, not everyone shares the same commitment to the team. Some team members will take the initiative, while others may be passive and need more encouragement and support. Each individual team member's dedication to team goals is important because accountability is shared. You need to be sure that team members understand—individually and collectively—how crucial it is for everyone to work toward a common goal.

How can you identify problem members and get a true picture of the inner workings of the team when you are, in a sense, on the outside looking in? Some individuals are natural-born leaders and others are followers, and you will soon recognize the leaders. Meet with one or two of them alone, informally, and ask for their honest assessment of the team's progress. Chances are the discussion eventually will turn to some of the problem areas and weaker members.

Also observe team members at progress meetings. Problem members are usually hesitant to speak up and often exhibit passive traits in their body language, such as averting their eyes, slouching, or appearing to be preoccupied.

STARTING OVER

A company-wide reorganization could wipe out some or all of your entire team. Although picking up the pieces after such upheaval is difficult, don't dwell on the negative. Instead, take a moment to reflect on your team's past successes. What you accomplished once, you can accomplish again.

Then determine with your manager what your new performance goals should be. You may be asked to join an entirely new team, or your manager may be able to help you put together a new team of your own.

Whatever happens, focusing on performance should always be your primary goal, because that is what will help you succeed personally.

THE BOTTOM LINE

Use the strategies and techniques discussed in earlier chapters, including frequent feedback, reviews, and coaching, to help improve the performance of weak team members.

Dealing with Underperforming Teams

The ideal management situation is to create a "high-performance team," which Katzenbach

---

The **BIG** Picture

CREATE A HIGH-PERFORMANCE TEAM

In *The Wisdom of Teams,* authors Katzenbach and Smith offer specific ways to turn a work group into a high-performance team:

- Create urgency and a sense of direction.

- Select team members based on their skills instead of personalities.

- Set up clear rules for members' behavior.

- Establish just a few immediate performance-oriented goals.

- Leverage the power of positive feedback, recognition, and reward.

SOURCE: *The Wisdom of Teams* by Jon R. Katzenbach and Douglas K. Smith (Harvard Business School Press, 1992).

---

and Smith define as consisting of members who are committed to each other's personal growth. A high-performance team can achieve far more than individuals working alone and can dramatically exceed your expectations.

But what happens if your team is less than stellar? What do you do if you find that your team is underperforming? To identify the problem, you need to consider the many possible reasons for lackluster performance.

> "Some of us will do our jobs well and some will not, but we will be judged by only one thing—the result."
>
> —Vince Lombardi, legendary NFL football coach

Leadership. Ask yourself a tough question: Are you an effective team leader? Have you clearly communicated the mission to the team? Are you managing your team properly by setting performance standards and monitoring progress?

Focus. Is your team focused on a common goal, or are they a group of individuals who don't seem to work together with one purpose?

Goals. Are the team's goals understandable, attainable, realistic, and measurable? Have you set a few specific performance-oriented goals stating what is needed, in what quantity, and by what date?

Skills. Does each team member have the skills the team needs and are they complementary? Are any team members lacking in necessary skills?

CASE *FILE*

ASK QUESTIONS

Asking questions is one of the best ways to find out how well your team is performing. When the great French general Napoleon Bonaparte wanted to find out what was going on with his troops, he would pretend he knew nothing about the situation and would ask question after question of everyone present. He wasn't afraid to appear ignorant. In fact, by the time he had absorbed all these experiences and observations, Napoleon was better informed than everyone else. What better way to find out what's truly happening with your team than asking lots of questions?

SOURCE: *Don't Fire Them, Fire Them Up* by Frank Pacetta (Simon & Schuster, 1994).

Cooperation. Do team members embrace a spirit of cooperation? Do they work collaboratively and toward a common goal without interpersonal conflicts? Are the individual team members' personalities compatible, and can they put differences aside for the benefit of the team?

Identifying the reasons for underperformance is the first step; the second step is finding a way

• POWER POINTS •

FIXING AN UNDERPERFORMING TEAM

To fix an underperforming team, you must first identify the problem. Is it a lack of leadership, focus, goals, skills, or cooperation? Then you need to:

- Concentrate on the problem area and try to get your team back on track.

- Understand what you really want your team to accomplish.

- Pick a single goal and get your team to complete it before moving on to another goal.

- Talk with the team to reinvigorate their sense of purpose.

- Meet with problem team members individually and get them to improve their performance.

to regroup and to get your team back on track. With a dysfunctional team, you need to spend more time managing with a defined purpose in mind. In other words, understand what you want your team to accomplish, and then determine the best way to get your team moving in the same direction.

You may want to concentrate on a single goal and make sure it is accomplished before moving on to the next goal. Consider having a heart-to-heart discussion with your team members to renew their sense of purpose. You also may need to meet with problem team members

Plan B

PREVENTING DEPARTURES

If a truly valuable team member asks for a transfer or wants to resign, try to avert this. Encourage a discussion of the reasons for the request, and ask what you can do to improve the situation. Appeal to the individual's commitment to the team and suggest that this departure will be detrimental to the team's success. Consider granting a promotion if it is warranted, or get permission from your manager to negotiate with the employee on salary or working conditions. These efforts may persuade the person to reconsider and stay on your team.

individually and set them straight. Use your best judgment and determine the most effective way to proceed.

DEALING WITH CHANGING ROLES

When a team is performing well, it is like a high-performance engine—all of the pistons are firing at just the right moment, the engine is humming along, and everything is running smoothly. But any disruption in the team's roles can slow that engine down.

> "Teams consist of many brains, with different expectations, fears, or filters."
>
> —David Rock,
> author of *Quiet Leadership*

In the normal course of business, changes are inevitable. For example, a team member may decide to resign, or someone may be transferred to another department. You may decide to promote a team member or have to terminate one.

Anything that affects a team member is likely to affect the performance of a team. Team members spend many hours working together and come to rely on each other to accomplish their goals. A truly effective team can suffer a setback when a member departs or changes roles—and that could hamper performance.

• POWER POINTS •

WHEN A TEAM MEMBER LEAVES

The departure of a team member changes the dynamic of a team, even if only temporarily. Be aware of its impact on the other members of the team and do the following:

- Begin the recruitment process as soon as you know a team member will be leaving.

- Let your team members know right away and involve them in recruiting a new team member.

- If performance issues led to the person's departure, help your team recognize that the team's performance will now improve.

- Reassess the remaining members' roles and responsibilities to decide if the departing member should be replaced, or if other team members can take over.

The Impact of a Team Member's Promotion on Performance

A team member's promotion can be a sensitive issue for the team in general and for individual members. As manager you want to recognize employees' contributions and give them the opportunity to advance. However, promoting a team member will immediately change the team dynamic. Former peers may now be expected to report to the promoted individual. Other team members might feel they have been passed over, or they may resent the promotion and, as a result, become less cooperative. If this happens, you need to minimize the personal impact of the promotion and rally your team members to continue to work together.

If necessary, meet with the employees who are most affected by the promotion and reassure them. Position the promotion as beneficial to the team. The other team members need to accept their colleague's promotion or they may lose their focus and performance will suffer.

The Impact of a Team Member's Departure on Performance

Don't underestimate the impact of a team member's departure on team performance. When a team member leaves, either by choice or by circumstance, the team dynamic can be seriously upset. As soon as you know about an impending departure, begin the recruitment process to replace the person. Get the rest of your team involved in recruitment so they can contribute to team management.

It is important to understand how the loss of that person will affect the overall performance of the team. If performance issues prompted the departure, your team members may see the event as positive, not negative. Help them recognize that the team's performance will now improve.

Sometimes the departure of a team member leads to a reassessment of the remaining team members' roles and responsibilities. Perhaps another team member is ready to take on the work of the departing employee, or perhaps the departing team member's role can be redefined and tasks redistributed. The team may become more efficient and achieve higher productivity because of the change.

Though a departure can be disruptive, view it as an opportunity to recommit your team to their performance goals.

IMPLEMENTING PERFORMANCE MANAGEMENT

> "Performance management can be defined as the ongoing communication between employee and supervisior that establishes clear expectations."
>
> —Robert Bacal,
> author of *Performance Management*

To evaluate the performance of individuals and teams effectively, more than just a method of individual appraisals is needed. Employee performance should be evaluated within the context of an organization-wide performance management system.

THE COMPONENTS OF PERFORMANCE MANAGEMENT

Most experts agree that a successful system of performance management involves four basic components: (1) a clear organizational definition of performance, (2) a training and development program that focuses on improving performance, (3) an objective evaluation system to review employee performance, and (4) a method of recognizing and rewarding performance.

Defining Performance

What is your definition of performance? Setting standards for employee performance is a crucial role of management. As an organization grows, departments and divisions tend to become less centralized. If a set of performance standards isn't defined early on, managers throughout the organization may not have clear, consistent guidelines for evaluating the performance of their employees.

While the organization can set overall performance standards, it is up to individual managers to develop them for their department or work group. This goal setting is essential. Only by setting specific, measurable, achievable, realistic, time-related goals can a manager establish meaningful performance standards.

Developing Performance-Oriented Employees

Employees may need training in basic skills to bring their level of competency up to an organization's performance standards. Advanced training in specialized subject areas will continue to improve their performance. Development isn't just about skills, however. Faced with a youthful, relatively inexperienced workforce, a manager's challenge today is to develop performance-oriented employees. Employees must understand and embrace the organization's performance standards. Training courses, motivational meetings, and individual coaching may help instill in them the desire to achieve and excel.

"In the zeal to measure and improve organizational performance, many organizations have paid scant attention to the developmental needs of their employees. Highly marketable employees value training and development and are no longer willing to forgo such opportunities."

—Elaine M. Evans,
author of *Compensation Basics for HR Generalists*

Evaluating Employee Performance

Once performance standards and goals have been defined, and performance development is in place, an employee evaluation system can be implemented. As discussed previously, this is an objective, comprehensive method of measuring employee performance. Evaluation systems include management by objectives (MBO), a rating scale (typically "Excellent" to "Poor"), narrative observations, including 360-degree feedback, or some combination of these methods. Formal evaluations are usually given on a regular schedule at least once a year or, ideally, more often; routinely offering informal performance evaluations of individual employees and teams should be encouraged, however.

Recognizing and Rewarding Performance

A wide variety of recognition and reward techniques can motivate employees to improve their performance, including informal positive reinforcement, periodic public recognition, bonuses, incentive compensation, travel or merchandise incentives, and promotions. What is used is less important than what it conveys.

Managers in the organization must be committed to the principle of performance-based benefits, and they must be sincere in giving recognition and rewards. While material rewards for major achievements can be effective, employees can also be motivated with a simple acknowledgment of a job well done. The organization should encourage both small and large forms of recognition to promote outstanding performance.

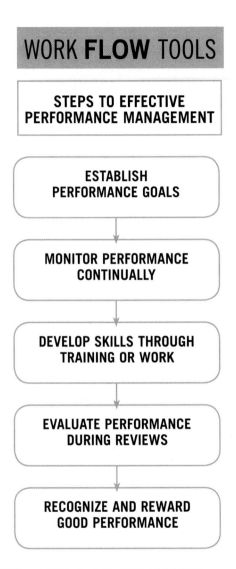

WORK **FLOW** TOOLS

STEPS TO EFFECTIVE PERFORMANCE MANAGEMENT

ESTABLISH PERFORMANCE GOALS

MONITOR PERFORMANCE CONTINUALLY

DEVELOP SKILLS THROUGH TRAINING OR WORK

EVALUATE PERFORMANCE DURING REVIEWS

RECOGNIZE AND REWARD GOOD PERFORMANCE

DEVELOPING A PERFORMANCE MANAGEMENT SYSTEM

The importance of performance management may seem obvious, yet most companies require

• POWER POINTS •

HOW TO EVALUATE PERFORMANCE

Evaluating an employee's performance is a serious responsibility. Evaluation methods vary from organization to organization. Managers must interpret their company guidelines correctly.

- Many companies use rating scales (1 to 5, A to F, etc.) that range from "Excellent" to "Poor."

- More and more companies are including 360-degree feedback—anonymous input from coworkers, customers, and suppliers.

- Some companies encourage managers to write narrative opinions.

- Other companies use management by objectives (MBO) to evaluate employee performance.

only an employee review process to manage performance. In the long term, this can be a fatal mistake.

If an organization isn't prepared to manage workforce performance comprehensively, it will quickly find itself at a competitive disadvantage. Today's businesses are largely information-based, which means it is the people they employ—and their ability to use information—that makes the difference.

Setting performance standards and developing the workforce's ability is crucial to a company's success. If an organization doesn't already have a performance management system in place, it should be a top priority. Senior management must be committed to the system, and the human resources department must develop it.

Behind the Numbers

IMPROVING PERFORMANCE MANAGEMENT

What are the biggest issues human resources executives face when it comes to employee performance management? Managers at organizations of three different sizes—small (under $50 million in sales), midsize ($50 million to $1 billion), and large (over $1 billion)—were surveyed. 61 percent of managers at all of the organizations surveyed said the top issue is attracting enough highly talented people. The second top issue among large organizations is that "competition is forcing us to increase employee productivity."

SOURCE: "The Employee Performance Management Benchmark Report," Aberdeen Group (June 2006).

CASE *FILE*

WHEN EMPLOYEES EVALUATE MANAGEMENT'S PERFORMANCE

Senior executives at a large manufacturing company were shocked when a corporate survey revealed that their employees were unhappy with the management styles and philosophy of the executive team. Instead of addressing the employees' concerns, however, the executive team published a watered-down version of the survey results, leaving out the criticism of their own performance.

When employees read the survey results, it was obvious to them that their opinions and suggestions had not been taken seriously. As a result, performance company-wide suffered even more.

Remember that when you solicit criticism of your management performance from your employees, you must accept their opinions, no matter how unwelcome. Listening to and acting on their suggestions to improve your own performance will result in a happier and more productive workforce.

SOURCE: *Gower Handbook of Internal Communication* by Eileen Scholes, ed. (Gower Publishing, 1997).

A quick-start approach might be to use the existing employee evaluation process as a jumping-off point. Defining performance, executing training and development, and implementing recognition and rewards can be based on that initial evaluation process, which can then be modified as needed.

> "We need to make sure we have the best people we can in our operations, and that is a constant challenge. There is always room to improve."
>
> —James Packer,
> Executive Chairman of Publishing
> and Broadcasting Limited

Applying Performance Management throughout the Organization

Managers must agree on the general performance standards for all employees, current and new. These performance standards should permeate the entire organization, but managers should also add their own standards based on their individual work group goals.

Training and development policies should be established, with guidelines for training requirements for all levels of employees. Managers should be provided with training tools and authorized to seek outside resources as needed.

Company management should devise a fair method for company-wide employee performance evaluation. While evaluations standards should be consistently applied to all employees, again, individual managers need to have some leeway in their evaluation criteria, based on their

CASE *FILE*

CONSTRUCTIVE CONFRONTATION

When Athlon Sports Publishing in Nashville, Tennessee, needed to improve its sales and production performance, then CEO Roger DiSilvestro engaged his people in a process of "constructive confrontation." The concept is simple and straightforward, but remarkably effective when followed consistently.

The approach requires managers and their direct reports to meet and break down specific jobs or projects into monthly, daily, and sometimes hourly tasks, then to document what everyone must do to support one another to get the work done. The manager then schedules

work group. Each manager should establish job descriptions and qualifications for new positions. To evaluate current employees, managers should add feedback from an employee's coworkers, suppliers, and customers, essential for a comprehensive and unbiased assessment.

Most companies use a performance rating scale of some sort. Rating scales are a convenient and manageable form of evaluation and can be applied objectively to a wide variety of positions and employees. They provide data in a form that can be easily analyzed and used.

The weakness of rating scales, however, is that they don't allow for individual variables. Sometimes rating someone "fair" or "very good"

a series of "constructive confrontations" in which the manager and direct report "confront," measure, and adjust the tasks as necessary. Finally, they celebrate progress and major accomplishments regularly.

Constructive confrontation is like performance appraisal on steroids. Every week performance is intensely evaluated, documented, and coached. The improvements in performance and productivity at Athlon broke all company records. Results have been consistent everywhere the program has been implemented.

SOURCE: *The Art of Constructive Confrontation* by John Hoover and Roger DiSilvestro (Wiley, 2005).

Plan B

ASKING EMPLOYEES WHAT THEY THINK MAY IMPROVE THEIR PERFORMANCE

The Donnelly Corporation believes in the value of employee surveys. The questions they suggest that you use are challenging—and hard not to want to answer. Ask questions like these, and you may find that they lead to improved employee performance:

- What made you mad today?

- What took too long?

- What was the cause of any complaints you fielded today?

- What misunderstandings have you encountered in the last week?

- What do you think costs too much?

- What waste have you seen around here lately?

- What procedures do we have that are too complicated?

SOURCE: *Reinventing Leadership* by Warren Bennis and Robert Townsend (Morrow, 1995).

doesn't provide enough information for a true picture of the individual's performance. For this reason, more companies now add narrative commentary about an employee's performance to the evaluation, prompted by specific questions or topics. While this requires a manager to spend more time on each evaluation, the added depth is valuable to both the company and the employee.

Finally, management should provide guidelines and policies for rewarding employees' efforts and achievements. Managers should have a menu of options so that they can reward and recognize each employee in the way that is most appropriate.

The Many Faces of Performance Evaluation

Evaluating employee performance is the focal point of most performance management systems. These common approaches consider the employee individually and in comparison to others in the work group.

Individual evaluation. Most managers are comfortable with evaluating an individual's performance based on common criteria, such as initiative, basic skills, ability to meet deadlines, and cooperation with coworkers. Evaluation methods include management by objectives, a rating scale or checklist, or a narrative approach. Typically, a manager doesn't compare the individual to others, but rates employees on their own merits.

Team evaluation. In team settings, a manager may be required to evaluate a team member in relation to other team members. Employees are "paired" and compared with each other. Typically, the manager selects the better-performing employee in each pairing.

Forced distribution. Forced distribution requires the manager to rank an employee according to categories that describe the ability of the workforce. For example, an employee may fall into the top 10 percent of workers, the middle 80 percent, or the bottom 10 percent. This type of ranking recognizes employees based on a "curve" rather than on individual merit. Recently the method has become controversial and has even been legally challenged.

Dos & Don'ts ☑

SETTING PERFORMANCE STANDARDS

Set rigorous organizational performance standards but allow managerial flexibility.

- ☐ Do agree on general performance standards that new and current employees must meet.

- ☐ Don't apply these standards without allowing managers the flexibility to add to or modify them based on their individual work group goals.

- ☐ Do provide managers with training tools to upgrade employees' performance.

- ☐ Don't restrict managers from establishing their own job descriptions and lists of necessary qualifications for positions in their work groups.

PERFORMANCE MANAGEMENT AS POLICY

Once a company institutes a performance management system, it must be maintained, reinforced, and modified with the times. This system should become the backbone of the company's human resources management, and all employees, customers, and shareholders should regard it as proof of the organization's dedication to improving performance.

☐ Do create a fair, objective method for company-wide performance evaluation.

☐ Do encourage managers to incorporate 360-degree feedback from coworkers, suppliers, and customers into employee evaluations.

☐ Don't employ a rating scale unless you are confident it accurately assesses individual performance.

☐ Do consider incorporating narrative commentary by managers into employee evaluations.

☐ Do provide guidelines for giving employees recognition and rewards.

EXEMPLARY PERFORMANCE MANAGEMENT
When the Gallup Organization interviewed exemplary managers to identify their secrets to performance management success, they found the following:

Great managers dislike complex evaluation processes – They don't like to waste time filling out bureaucratic forms, preferring a simple process that focuses on communicating clearly with their employees.

Great managers interact frequently with their employees – Yearly or semi-yearly

Organizations would do well to make performance management a company policy and keep employees aware of it in several ways.

A company should hold an annual meeting during which the most important company policies are reviewed. All new employees should also be briefed at orientation sessions. Whenever a policy is updated, a memo detailing the changes should be distributed to all employees. An important update could even warrant a special meeting.

Managers must must make sure their teams are aware of the company policies that affect them. When managers take a company policy seriously, so will employees.

Plan B

performance appraisals don't cut it, as far as these managers are concerned; employees need constant and consistent feedback.

Great managers focus on the future – While they refer to past performance on occasion, they primarily concentrate on where the company is going and the results that need to be achieved to get there.

SOURCE: *First Break All the Rules* by Marcus Buckingham and Curt Coffman (Simon & Schuster, 1999).

Training Managers to Evaluate Performance

A performance management policy is of little use if managers don't know how to evaluate their staff. Every manager should be trained to evaluate performance—how to identify and handle underperforming employees and teams, provide frequent feedback, assess individual progress, review employees effectively, and reward achievement. Effective performance management is only as good as the managers who implement it.

Employees' Legal Rights

Some methods of employee evaluation appear to have merit from a company's perspective, but

could be interpreted by employees as unfair—
and potentially illegal. "Forced distribution,"
described earlier, is one example.

Employees' legal rights must be taken into
account in the performance evaluation and

• POWER POINTS •

MAKING PERFORMANCE MANAGEMENT A POLICY

Implementing a performance management system is the first step toward
making it a company policy.

- A performance management system
  must be maintained, reinforced,
  and modified with the times.

- Performance management is most
  effective as a company policy.

- As a company policy, performance
  management should be reviewed at
  the company's annual meeting and
  introduced to new employees during orientation sessions.

- Managers should be trained to evaluate performance: how to deal with
  underperforming employees, offer
  feedback, assess progress, conduct
  reviews, and provide recognition
  and rewards.

management process. While a manager has every right to evaluate the performance of an employee, that evaluation must be objective, fair, and unbiased. Any evaluation that can be interpreted in any way as discriminatory can cause a company considerable legal problems.

> "Nothing challenges men as effectively to improved performance as a job that makes high demands on them...It is equally important that management set and enforce on itself high standards for its own performance."
>
> —Peter Drucker

This is why it is critical to be aware of federal and local laws regarding employees' legal rights when you implement performance management systems and train managers to do employee reviews. Consider the following equal employment opportunity (EEO) laws, which prohibit specific types of job discrimination in certain workplaces and protect employees against discrimination on the grounds of age, disability, ethnic or national origin, color, race, religion, sex, or status as a veteran:

Title VII of the Civil Rights Act of 1964. Title VII prohibits employment discrimination based on race, color, religion, sex, or national origin. When you evaluate an employee's performance, approve or deny a raise or promotion, or take

The BIG Picture

THE ONE TO LIVE BY

The most important set of federal laws are the Equal Employment Opportunity (EEO) laws prohibiting discrimination in the workplace.

Managers must understand that any form of discrimination on the basis of age, race, religion, sex, origin, or disability is illegal. A manager who unwittingly asks personal questions of an employee during a job interview, a performance review, or even in casual conversation can be vulnerable to a claim of discrimination.

Evaluating employee performance is the manager's right, but it must be done objectively, fairly, and without bias to avoid the risk of legal action by a disgruntled employee.

Dos & Don'ts ☑

EMPLOYEE RIGHTS

Your human resources department can help you interpret all the various laws and regulations that may affect your workplace. Meanwhile, here are some basic guidelines:

- ☐ Do be aware of federal, state, and local laws governing employee rights.

- ☐ Do seek guidance from your human resources department before making any hiring and firing decisions.

- ☐ Don't terminate an employee with performance problems unless you have legitimate business reasons and just cause.

- ☐ Do deal fairly with all employees, especially during employee reviews, without regard to race, religion, sex, origin, or disability.

- ☐ Don't ask any personal questions of an employee that could result in a claim of discrimination.

- ☐ Don't make employment decisions based on an individual's personal life or financial status.

any disciplinary action, be sure that you do so solely on the individual's performance and without discriminating against that employee.

Equal Pay Act of 1963. EPA protects men and women who perform substantially equal work in the same establishment from gender-biased wage discrimination. When you evaluate an employee's performance, award merit increases or promotions only on the basis of achievement. Don't allow gender to influence a pay increase or a promotion.

Age Discrimination in Employment Act of 1967. ADEA protects individuals who are 40 years of age or older from discrimination. Any action you take with an employee 40 years of age or older, whether it is hiring, firing, demoting, or promoting, should be based solely on performance, not age.

Title I and Title V of the Americans with Disabilities Act of 1990; Sections 501 and 505 of the Rehabilitation Act of 1973. The ADA prohibits employment discrimination against qualified individuals with disabilities in the private sector and in state and local governments; Sections 501 and 505 address the federal government. Be sure when you evaluate an individual's performance that you don't unintentionally discriminate against an employee with a disability.

ASSESSING THE EFFECTIVENESS OF PERFORMANCE MANAGEMENT

One major advantage of performance management is that it allows the organization to measure its impact on the business. A clear sign of effectiveness is the quality of the workforce.

If a performance management system is effective, a company will see marked improvement in its workforce, including a higher retention rate, productivity, employee morale, levels of competency, and percentage of employee advancement.

CASE *FILE*

PERFORMANCE SUFFERS WHEN COMPENSATION POLICIES CHANGE

In the late 1980s, Andersen Consulting (now Accenture) started to hire outside strategy consultants to improve the performance of its core IT business. When the new hires asked to be paid what they had received from their former employers, Andersen's other employees complained, so Andersen modified its compensation system in an attempt to satisfy the new employees' demands without alienating the employees who had been hired previously. Andersen also tried to force-fit the new employees into its existing staff structure. Both efforts at integrating the new consultants failed. Many of them quit, and Andersen's attempt at building the new business was unsuccessful.

SOURCE: "Employee Incentive Systems," Knowledge@Wharton (May 31, 2006).

The company will attract and retain higher-quality managers as well.

A company should regularly reassess its performance management standards to ensure that they remain current and suitable for the makeup and demands of its workplace. Progressive companies solicit employee opinions on performance evaluation standards via surveys and company meetings. Inviting employees to help set standards makes for a more motivated, empowered workforce.

Managers should review organizational performance standards with all employees, not just

Behind the Numbers

IMPROVING PERFORMANCE: WHAT EMPLOYEES AND EMPLOYERS THINK

Only three in ten employees thought their companies' performance review system actually improved performance, according to a 2006 study conducted by Watson Wyatt, a human resources consulting organization. In another Watson Wyatt study, almost half of the employers surveyed reported that they thought their managers were only slightly effective in helping underperforming employees to improve.

SOURCE: "Performance Reviews: Many Need Improvement" by Kelley Holland, *New York Times* (September 10, 2006).

new ones. This is an opportunity to discuss the organization's rating system, 360-degree feedback, the review process, and the importance of an objective evaluation.

The **BIG** Picture

PERFORMANCE MANAGEMENT CONTRARIANS

Not all company managers believe they should be responsible for continually advising and guiding employees in an effort to improve their performance. Scott Flanders, CEO of California-based Freedom Communications, thinks managers shouldn't waste precious time holding employees' hands. "We can't tolerate mediocrity, but we have to presume the competence of employees—and then, when we're disappointed, spend time coaching and training," he says. According to *The Wall Street Journal,* it's a trend that managers must learn to live with because, in many cases, "they are expected to produce work themselves while supervising employees' output."

SOURCE: "Today's Bosses Find Mentoring Isn't Worth the Time and Risks" by Carolyn Hymowitz, *Wall Street Journal* (March 13, 2006).

HOW TO MEASURE PERFORMANCE MANAGEMENT EFFECTIVENESS

Key metrics for measuring performance management effectiveness include:

- Year-over-year changes in employee competency ratings

- Percent of available positions filled from within the company

- Average performance rating per business unit

- Percent of improvement in employee satisfaction

- Employee retention rate

- Number of cross-functional teams utilized

- Ability to meet business process improvement targets

SOURCE: "Getting There: The Business Benefits of Workforce Performance Management," SuccessFactors.com (September 2005).

THE BOTTOM LINE

It is important for employees to feel that performance standards are beneficial to them, not just to the company. Employees need to see that evaluating performance is a means of ensuring that all

• POWER POINTS •

IS PERFORMANCE MANAGEMENT EFFECTIVE?

There are a few things you can do to ensure your performance management policies remain current and effective:

- Measure improvements in retention rate, productivity, employee morale, competency level, and employee advancement.

- Regularly reassess performance standards to make sure you are keeping up with the demands of the workplace.

- Encourage employees to comment on performance evaluation standards. This makes for a motivated, empowered workforce.

employees are held to the same high standard. If employees believe that performance standards help managers recognize and reward good workers—and identify and eliminate sub-par workers—they will strive to do their best, perform at their optimum level, and ultimately contribute to their organization's success.

Off and Running >>>

You are now ready to put what you have learned from this book into practice. Use this section as a review guide.

CHAPTER 1.
ONE-ON-ONE PERFORMANCE MANAGEMENT

- Do your homework: You won't know what the most important qualities of an employee are until you've sat down and reworked the job description to meet your needs.

- Start by hiring the right people: While it's tempting to chose the best three resumes and make a quick decision after a brief meeting, interviewing more candidates will pay off when you find your dream employee.

- Create SMART goals, objectives that are Specific, Measurable, Achievable, Realistic, and Time-related.

- Self-evaluation can be an important tool that lets employees examine their own habits and behavior.

CHAPTER 2.
PROMOTING EMPLOYEES

- A promotion isn't merely a change in job title; it should result in an increase in responsibility and authority.

- Promoting from within shows employees that the company offers advancement opportunities.

- Rather than a promotion, offer incentives to an employee you don't want to lose—a higher salary, a more flexible work schedule, or better benefits.

- A promotion should not be a reward for a one-time achievement; give a bonus instead.

CHAPTER 3.
DEALING WITH UNDERPERFORMERS

- Don't rely solely on secondhand information; retain your objectivity and give the employee the benefit of the doubt.

- If you have an issue with an employee underperforming or doing something wrong, take it up in private, not in front of everybody.

Off and Running >>>

- Sometimes you can only do so much; if an employee has personal problems, it might be best to sit back and listen and empathize rather than offer a solution. Suggest seeking professional help.

- Keep good records and keep your cool: Even an oral reprimand should be noted in the employee's file. Also remain calm and be firm yet fair in explaining your assertions. Allow the employee to respond, but maintain your position.

- Sometimes you have the wrong person doing the wrong job; redeploying this person to a better-fitting position often results in a win-win situation.

- Get closure in writing: A terminated employee should review his or her termination letter and sign and date it.

- Retirement doesn't have to mean good-bye: Employees who continue working past retirement age, whether as part-timers or consultants, promote company loyalty and stability and make economic sense.

CHAPTER 4.
EVALUATING TEAM PERFORMANCE

- Build team spirit: Get all team members to help set goals so that everybody feels a common purpose and collective ownership.

- If it's broke, fix it: If a team is underperforming, objectively identify the problem. Is it your leadership? Lack of focus? Unclear goals? Missing skill sets? Miscommunication?

- Diagnose the problem, then get your team back on track.

- An employee's departure provides an opportune time to evaluate the team and involve the remaining members to reassess their roles and responsibilities.

CHAPTER 5.
IMPLEMENTING PERFORMANCE MANAGEMENT

- The best corporate management policies provide clear definitions, training and development, objective evaluation, and a rewards system.

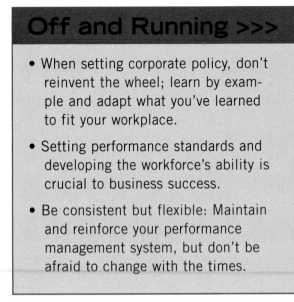

Off and Running >>>

- When setting corporate policy, don't reinvent the wheel; learn by example and adapt what you've learned to fit your workplace.

- Setting performance standards and developing the workforce's ability is crucial to business success.

- Be consistent but flexible: Maintain and reinforce your performance management system, but don't be afraid to change with the times.

- Follow the law: Educate yourself about the laws and regulations concerning the equal treatment of employees, and be sensitive to unconscious discrimination.

- Periodically review organizational performance standards with all employees, not just new ones.

Recommended Reading

The Transparent Leader: How to Build a Great Company Through Straight Talk, Openness, and Accountability
Herb Baum with Tammy Kling
In the wake of numerous corporate scandals, Baum offers business leaders a compelling method to get maximum results by being open and honest in business practices.

Leaders: Strategies for Taking Charge, 2nd ed.
Warren Bennis and Burt Nanus
Leadership guru Warren Bennis and his coauthor Burt Nanus reveal the four key principles every manager should know.

Organizing Genius: The Secrets of Creative Collaboration
Warren Bennis and Patricia Ward Biederman
Bennis and Biederman explain how the sum can equal more than the parts of the whole when team members successfully collaborate. Real-life examples give dimension to the authors' anecdotes and analysis.

Reinventing Leadership: Strategies to Empower the Organization
Warren Bennis and Robert Townsend
Two of America's foremost experts on leadership show how their strategies can lead organizations into a future that includes increased employee satisfaction and continued economic growth.

*Leadership and the One Minute Manager: Increasing
Effectiveness through Situational Leadership®*
Ken Blanchard with Patricia Zigarmi and Drea Zigarmi
Best-selling author Blanchard teaches managers how to use
his patented method of Situational Leadership®—a system
that refutes the conventional management mandate of treating
all employees equally—and how to elicit the best performance
from employees.

The One Minute Manager Builds High Performing Teams
Ken Blanchard, Eunice Parisi-Carew, and Donald Carew
Blanchard and company show how to develop any group into a
high-performing team with efficiency and minimal stress.

*First, Break All the Rules: What the World's Greatest Managers
Do Differently*
Marcus Buckingham and Curt Coffman
This book presents four management keys that will help you
do a better job of hiring, evaluating, promoting, and, if necessary, firing employees. The author advocates finding the right
fit for employees, focusing on their strengths, defining desired
results, and selecting people with talent.

*The Success Principles™: How to Get from Where You Are to
Where You Want to Be*
Jack Canfield with Janet Switzer
One of the coauthors of the incredibly successful *Chicken
Soup for the Soul* series provides the principles and strategies
to meet a wide variety of goals.

Integrity: The Courage to Meet the Demands of Reality
Henry Cloud
Dr. Cloud explores the six qualities of character that define
integrity. He uses stories from well-known business leaders and
sports figures to illustrate each of these qualities.

*Good to Great: Why Some Companies Make the Leap . . . and
Others Don't*
Jim Collins
The findings from *Good to Great* will surprise many readers
and shed light on virtually every area of management strategy
and practice.

*Monday Morning Mentoring: Ten Lessons to Guide You
Up the Ladder*
David Cottrell
In this inspirational book, Cottrell shows how your success as
a manager is intimately bound up with the success of your
people. He demonstrates that tolerating lackluster performance
in yourself and others on the team leads to discontent among
your most prized and productive employees.

*Turned On: Eight Vital Insights to Energize Your People,
Customers, and Profits*
Roger J. Dow
Turned On explains how managers can let their employees take
control of their jobs, think in new ways, and find common-
sense solutions to seemingly insurmountable challenges.

*The Daily Drucker: 366 Days of Insight and Motivation for
Getting the Right Things Done*
Peter F. Drucker with Joseph A. Maciariello
Widely regarded as the greatest management thinker of modern
times, Drucker here offers his penetrating and practical wis-
dom with his trademark clarity, vision, and humanity.
The Daily Drucker provides the inspiration and advice to
meet life's many challenges.

The Effective Executive
Peter F. Drucker
Drucker shows how to "get the right things done," demonstrat-
ing the distinctive skill of the executive and offering fresh
insights into old and seemingly obvious business situations.

Innovation and Entrepreneurship
Peter F. Drucker
This is the classic business tome for presenting innovation and
entrepreneurship as a purposeful and systematic discipline.
This practical book explains what all businesses and institu-
tions have to know, learn, and do in today's market.

The Practice of Management
Peter F. Drucker
The first book to depict management as a distinct function and
to recognize managing as a separate responsibility, this classic
Drucker work is the fundamental and basic book for under-
standing these ideas.

Why Employees Don't Do What They're Supposed to Do and What to Do About It
Ferdinand F. Fournies
This *New York Times* business best-seller identifies the top ten reasons employees don't do what they're supposed to do and presents simple yet effective strategies for handling each one.

Corps Business: The 30 Management Principles of the U.S. Marines
David H. Freedman
Freedman examines the organization and culture of the United States Marine Corps and relates how business enterprises could benefit from such Marine values as sacrifice, perseverance, integrity, commitment, and loyalty.

The E-Myth Manager: Why Most Managers Aren't Effective and What to Do About It
Michael E. Gerber
Drawing on lessons learned from working with more than 15,000 small, medium-sized, and very large organizations, Gerber reveals why management doesn't work—and what to do about it.

What Really Works: The 4+2 Formula for Sustained Business Success
William Joyce, Nitin Nohria, and Bruce Roberson
Based on a groundbreaking 5-year study, analyzing data on 200 management practices gathered over a 10-year period, *What Really Works* reveals the effectiveness of practices that really matter.

The Wisdom of Teams: Creating the High Performance Organization
Jon R. Katzenbach and Douglas K. Smith
Authors Katzenbach and Smith reveal what is the most important element in team success, who excels at team leadership, and why companywide change depends on teams.

Swim with the Sharks without Being Eaten Alive: Outsell, Outmanage, Outmotivate, and Outnegotiate Your Competition
Harvey B. Mackay
In this straight-from-the-hip handbook, with almost 2 million in print, best-selling author and self-made millionaire Mackay reviews the secrets of his success.

You Can't Win a Fight with Your Boss: & 55 Other Rules for Success
Tom Markert
This guide to surviving the pitfalls of the modern corporate environment presents 56 practical rules that one can use to find corporate success.

Executive Intelligence: What All Great Leaders Have
Justin Menkes
In this thought-provoking volume, Menkes pinpoints the cognitive skills needed to thrive in senior management positions.

The Corporate Coach: How to Build a Team of Loyal Customers and Happy Employees
James B. Miller with Paul B. Brown
Founder and CEO of Miller Business Systems, Jim Miller shows how giving customers legendary services and also motivating employees makes for a winning combination.

Stop Whining—and Start Winning: Recharging People, Re-Igniting Passion, and Pumping Up Profits
Frank Pacetta
This upbeat book offers managers who are fed up with their worker's ho-hum attitude a no-fail formula for ending the whining and instilling in managers and employees a winning spirit.

The HP Way: How Bill Hewlett and I Built Our Company
David Packard
David Packard and Bill Hewlett grew their company from its start in a one-car garage to a multibillion-dollar industry. Here is the story of the vision, innovation, and hard work that built an empire.

In Search of Excellence: Lessons from America's Best-Run Companies
Thomas J. Peters and Robert H. Waterman, Jr.
Based on a study of 43 of America's best-run companies from a diverse array of business sectors, *In Search of Excellence* describes eight basic principles of management that made these organizations successful.

Quiet Leadership: Six Steps to Transforming Performance at Work
David Rock
Rock demonstrates how to be a quiet leader—and a master at bringing out the best performance in others—by improving the way people process information.

The Cycle of Leadership: How Great Leaders Teach Their Companies to Win
Noel M. Tichy
Using examples from real companies, Tichy shows how managers can begin to transform their own businesses into teaching organizations and, consequently, better-performing companies with better-performing employees.

The Leadership Engine: How Winning Companies Build Leaders at Every Level
Noel M. Tichy
A framework for developing leaders at all levels of an organization helps to develop the next generation of leaders so that a company can grow from within, which is the key to excellence, stability, and building team loyalty.

Ten Steps to Empower: A Common-Sense Guide to Managing People
Diane Tracy
This straightforward book shows how empowering employees is key to maximum productivity, maintaining employee morale, and meeting the long-term objectives of the company.

It's Okay to Be the Boss: The Step-by-Step Guide to Becoming the Manager Your Employees Need
Bruce Tulgan
Tulgan advocates a hands-on approach to managing, suggesting managers must set clear expectations and goals for their employees, monitor their progress, provide regular feedback, deal quickly with underperformers, and reward high performance appropriately.

The Visionary's Handbook: Nine Paradoxes That Will Shape the Future of Your Business
Watts Wacker and Jim Taylor with Howard Means
This book presents a vision of the present and future to create a course for the future based upon the authors' understanding of nine paradoxes that define the world's business and social climates.

Winning
Jack Welch with Suzy Welch
The core of *Winning* is devoted to the real "stuff" of work. Packed with personal anecdotes, this book offers deep insights, original thinking, and solutions to nuts-and-bolts problems.

Index

Make sure you have all the Best Practices!

Make sure you have all the Best Practices!

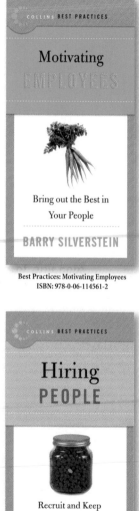